JAPANESE
In Your Pocket

NH
NEW HOLLAND

GLOBETROTTER™

First edition published in 2009
by New Holland Publishers Ltd
London • Cape Town • Sydney
• Auckland
10 9 8 7 6 5 4 3 2 1

website:
www.newhollandpublishers.com

Garfield House, 86 Edgware Road
London W2 2EA
United Kingdom

80 McKenzie Street
Cape Town 8001
South Africa

Unit 1, 66 Gibbes Street
Chatswood, NSW 2067
Australia

218 Lake Road
Northcote, Auckland
New Zealand

Copyright © 2009 in text: Yasuhiro Ueda
Copyright © 2009 in photograph: Pictures Colour Library
Copyright © 2009 in illustrations: Marisa Roman
Copyright © 2009 New Holland Publishers (UK) Ltd

ISBN 978 1 84537 574 4

All rights reserved. No part of this publication may be reproduced, stored in a retrieval system or transmitted, in any form or by any means, electronic, mechanical, photocopying, recording or otherwise, without the prior written permission of the publishers and copyright holders.

Although every effort has been made to ensure that this guide is correct at time of going to print, the Publisher accepts no responsibility or liability for any loss, injury or inconvenience incurred by readers or travellers using this guide.

Publishing Manager: Thea Grobbelaar
Designer: Lellyn Creamer
Cover Design: Nicole Bannister
Illustrator: Marisa Roman
Editor: Carla Zietsman
Translator: Yasuhiro Ueda
Proofreaders: Mika Gorton and Koji Hasnoname

Reproduction by Resolution, Cape Town
Printed and bound by Replika Press, India

Cover photograph:
Ginza, an up-market suburb of Tokyo, is a designer shopping destination.

CONTENTS

PHRASE BOOK

	Introduction	4
	How to use this book	6
	Pronunciation	8
	Grammar	14
	Basics	20
	Transport	28
	Accommodation	40
	Eating and Drinking	48
	Money and Shopping	58
	Activities	66
	Health and Safety	72
	Etiquette	78
	Holidays and Festivals	82

DICTIONARY

	English – Japanese	86
	Japanese – English	140

INTRODUCTION

This PHRASE BOOK is thematically colour-coded for easy use and is organized according to the situation you're most likely to be in when you need it. The fairly comprehensive DICTIONARY section consists of two parts – English/Japanese and Japanese/English.

To make speaking Japanese easy, we encourage our readers to memorize some general PRONUNCIATION rules (*see* page 8). After you have familiarized yourself with the basic tools of the language and the rudiments of Japanese GRAMMAR (*see* page 14), all you need to do is turn to the appropriate section of the phrase book and find the words you need to make yourself understood. If the selection is not exactly what you're looking for, consult the dictionary for other options.

Just to get you started, you are bound to be familiar with a few Japanese words such as sushi, bonsai, kamikaze **and** kimono. Even if you are unfamiliar with these words and would rather

はじめに

not try to say them out loud, just remain confident, follow our easy advice and practise a little, and you will soon master useful phrases for everyday life. Speak slowly and enunciate carefully and your counterpart is likely to follow suit.

Nowadays many English words are used in Japanese, but the pronunciations are usually changed to suit the Japanese language. For instance the word 'hotel' becomes hoteru.

A section on HOLIDAYS AND FESTIVALS (*see* page 82) provides some background knowledge so that you know what you're celebrating and why. There's no better way to learn a language than joining in some enjoyment!

The brief section on manners, mannerisms and ETIQUETTE (*see* page 78) can help you make sense of the people around you. Make an effort to view your host country and its people tolerantly – that way you will be open to the new experience and able to enjoy it.

HOW TO USE THIS BOOK

Learning a new language can be a wonderful but frightening experience. It is not the object of this book to teach you perfect Japanese, but rather to equip you with just enough knowledge for a successful holiday or business trip. Luckily you are unlikely to be criticized on your grammatical correctness when merely asking for directions. The most important thing is to make yourself understood. To this end a brief section on grammar and a guide to pronunciation have been included in this book. There is, however, no substitute for listening to native speakers.

Before you leave, it might be a good idea to familiarize yourself with the sections on Pronunciation, Grammar and Etiquette. This can easily be done en route to your destination. You will also benefit from memorizing a few important phrases before you go.

The sections of the Phrase Book are arranged by topic for quick reference. Simply go to the contents list (*see* page 3) to find the topic you need. The Dictionary section (*see* page 86) goes both ways, helping you to understand and be understood.

HOW TO USE THIS BOOK

Abbreviations have been used in those instances where one English word could be interpreted as more than one part of speech, e.g. 'smoke' (a noun, the substance coming from a fire) and 'smoke' (a verb, what one would do with a cigarette). Here is a list of these and some other abbreviations used in this book:

vb	verb
n	noun
adj	adjective
adv	adverb
elec	electric/al
rel	religion

For ease of reference, the Japanese–English section of the dictionary (*see* page 140) has been alphabetized according to the transliteration rather than according to the Japanese characters.

PRONUNCIATION

TONES 9
音色 neiro

VOWELS 9
母音 boin

CONSONANTS 10
子音 shiin

HOW TO PRONOUNCE 10
発音の仕方 hatsuon no shikata

発音

THE TONES
音色 neiro

Japanese is not a tonal language like Chinese or Thai, and is comparatively easy to pronounce.

VOWELS
母音 boin

The vowels **a**, **e**, **i**, **o**, and **u** are generally pronounced somewhat similarly to those in Spanish.

♦ The vowel **u** is similar to that of the **oo** in **moon**, although shorter and without lip-rounding. In certain contexts, such as after **s** at the end of a word, the vowel is devoiced, so **desu** may sound like **dess**.

♦ Japanese vowels can either be long (bimoraic) or short (monomoraic).

Japanese vowels can be approximated in English as follows:

Vowel	a	i	u	e	o
British Received Pronunciation	between cap and cup	as in feet	as in boot	as in hey	as in dog
General American	as in father	as in feet	as in boot	as in hey	as in old

PRONUNCIATION

CONSONANTS
子音 shiin

◆ Consonants other than **f** and **r** are generally pronounced as in English.
◆ The consonant **f** is bilabial: the teeth are not used, and the sound is much softer than the **f** of English.
◆ The consonant **r** is similar to Korean r. To an English speaker's ears, its pronunciation lies somewhere between a flapped **t** (as in American and Australian English **better** and **ladder**), an **l** and a **d**. Double consonants (**kk**, **tt**, etc.) basically indicate a slight, sharp pause before and stronger emphasis of the following sound, more similar to Italian than English.

HOW TO PRONOUNCE
発音の仕方 hatsuon no shikata

Japanese Characters (ひらがな hiragana)					
	a	**i**	**u**	**e**	**o**
	あ	い	う	え	お
k	か	き	く	け	こ
s	さ	し	す	せ	そ
t	た	(ち)	(つ)	て	と
n	な	に	ぬ	ね	の
h	は	ひ	ふ	へ	ほ

発音

m	ま	み	む	め	も
y	や		ゆ		よ
r	ら	り	る	れ	ろ
w	わ				を
	ん (n)				
g	が	ぎ	ぐ	げ	ご
z	ざ	じ	ず	ぜ	ぞ
d	だ	(ぢ)	(づ)	で	ど
b	ば	び	ぶ	べ	ぼ
p	ぱ	ぴ	ぷ	ぺ	ぽ
ky	きゃ		きゅ		きょ
sy	しゃ		しゅ		しょ
ty	(ちゃ)		(ちゅ)		(ちょ)
hy	ひゃ		ひゅ		ひょ
gy	ぎゃ		ぎゅ		ぎょ
zy	じゃ		じゅ		じょ
by	びゃ		びゅ		びょ
ch	ちゃ	ち	ちゅ		ちょ
j	じゃ	じ	じゅ		じょ
sh	しゃ	し	しゅ		しょ
ts			つ		
f			ふ		

PRONUNCIATION

Japanese Pronunciation: Vowels

a あ/ア like the **a** in **father**

i い/イ like the **i** in **machine**

u う/ウ like the **oo** in **hoop**

e え/エ like **e** in **set**

o お/オ like **o** in **rope**

n ん/ン short **n** at the end of a syllable, pronounced as **m** before **b**, **p** or **m**.

Note that **u** is often weak at the end of syllables. In particular, the common endings **-desu** and **-masu** are pronounced as **dess** and **mass** respectively.

Japanese Pronunciation: Consonants

k like **k** in **king**

g like the **g** in **go**

s like the **s** in **sit**

z like the **z** in **haze**

t like the **t** in **top**

発音

d like the **d** in dog

n like the **n** in nice

h like the **h** in **help**

p like the **p** in pig

b like the **b** in bed

m like the **m** in mother

y like the **y** in yard

r like the **r** in **row** (actually a sound between l and r, but closer to r)

w like the **w** in wall

ch (**t** before **i**) like **ch** in touch

sh (**s** before **i**) like **sh** in sheep

ts (**t** before **u**) like **ts** in hot soup

f (**h** before **u**) like **f** in far

j (**d** before **i**) like **j** in jar

GRAMMAR

OUTLINE 15
概要 gaiyo

NOUNS 16
名詞 meishi

PRONOUNS 16
代名詞 daimeishi

VERBS 17
動詞 doshi

ADJECTIVES 18
形容詞 keiyoshi

TEXTUAL CLASSIFICATIONS 19
文の区分 bun no kubun

文法

The grammar section has deliberately been kept very brief as this is not a language course.

OUTLINE
概要 gaiyo

The Japanese language has a highly regular agglutinative (process of adding affixes to the base of a word) verb structure, with both productive and fixed elements. According to linguistic classifications, its most prominent feature is topic creation: Japanese has prominent topics (although it is possible for topics and subjects to be distinct). Grammatically, Japanese is an SOV (Subject Object Verb type of language in which the subject, object, and verb of a sentence appear or usually appear in that order) dependent-marking language, with verbs always constrained to the sentence-final position, except in some rhetorical and poetic usage. Japanese is a typical example of almost pure dependent marking, where each part of a sentence is supposed to be marked for its function (topic, subject, object, complement), while the verb has no

GRAMMAR

structural indicators showing person, number, gender, or any other property of the arguments.

NOUNS
名詞 meishi

Japanese has no grammatical gender, number, or articles. Nouns are non-inflecting: 犬 (inu) can be translated as 'dog', 'dogs', 'a dog', 'the dog', 'some dogs' and so forth, depending on context. Japanese nouns do not change to show politeness or respect. Generally, the prefix o- for native nouns, and go- for Sino-Japanese nouns, serves to make the noun polite.

PRONOUNS
代名詞 daimeishi

Japanese lacks true pronouns. Daimeishi (pronouns) can be viewed as a subset of nouns. Japanese de-emphasizes personal daimeishi (pronouns), which are seldom used. This is partly because Japanese sentences do not always require explicit subjects, and partly because names or titles are often used where pronouns would appear in a translation:

上田さんは、背が高いですね。
Ueda-san wa, se ga takai desu ne.
(addressing Mr. Ueda) 'You're pretty tall, aren't you?'

VERBS
動詞 doshi

Verbs in Japanese are situated at the ends of clauses in what is known as the predicate position.

犬	は	肉	を	食べる。
inu	wa	Meat	o	Taberu
Dogs	TOPIC	Meat	OBJECT	Eat

Dogs eat meat.

The subject and objects of the verb are indicated by means of particles. The grammatical functions of the verb are indicated by means of conjugation. When the subject and the dissertative topic coincide, the subject is often omitted;

if the verb is intransitive, the entire sentence may consist of a single verb. Verbs have two tenses past and nonpast, indicated by conjugation. The difference between present and future is not indicated by means of conjugation. Usually there is no confusion because few verbs can operate in both uses.

ADJECTIVES
形容詞 keiyoshi

Japanese has two main classes of adjectives:
- i-adjectives (形容詞 keiyoshi) – these are very similar to verbs.
- na-adjectives (形容動詞 keiyodoshi, lit. 'Adjectival verb') – these are nouns that are altered with the linking verb to form adjectives.

Unlike adjectives in English, adjectives in Japanese change according to aspect and mood, like verbs. Japanese adjectives do not have comparative or superlative modifications.

This is indicated by using adverbs like もっと (motto, **more**) and 一番 (ichiban, **most**).

TEXTUAL CLASSIFICATIONS
文の区分 bun no kubun

Text (文章 bunsho) is composed of sentences (文 bun), which are composed of phrases (文節 bunsetsu), which are its smallest understandable parts. Written Japanese does not typically demarcate words with spaces. Word divisions are indicated by semantic cues and knowledge of phrase structure. Phrases contain a single meaning-bearing word, followed by a string of suffixes, auxiliary verbs and particles to modify its meaning and indicate its grammatical role. In the following example, bunsetsu (**phrases**) are indicated by vertical bars:

太陽が｜東の｜空に｜昇る。
Taiyo ga | higashi no | sora ni | noboru
sun SUBJECT | east POSSESSIVE | sky LOCATIVE | rise
The sun rises in the eastern sky.

BASICS

NUMBERS 21
数 kazu

DAYS 22
日にち hinichi

MONTHS 22
月 tsuki

TIME 23
時間 jikan

GREETINGS 24
挨拶 aisatsu

GENERAL 25
一般 ippan

FORMS AND SIGNS 26
用紙とサイン yoshi to sain

基本

NUMBERS
数 kazu

- **0** 0 zero
- **1** 1 ichi
- **2** 2 ni
- **3** 3 san
- **4** 4 shi / yon
- **5** 5 go
- **6** 6 roku
- **7** 7 shichi / nana
- **8** 8 hachi
- **9** 9 kyu / ku
- **10** 10 jyu
- **11** 11 jyu ichi
- **12** 12 jyu ni
- **13** 13 jyu san
- **14** 14 jyu shi / jyu yon
- **15** 15 jyu go
- **16** 16 jyu roku
- **17** 17 jyu shichi / jyu nana
- **18** 18 jyu hachi
- **19** 19 jyu ku
- **20** 20 nijyu
- **21** 21 nijyu ichi
- **22** 22 nijyu ni
- **30** 30 sanjyu
- **40** 40 yonjyu
- **50** 50 gojyu
- **60** 60 rokujyu
- **70** 70 nanajyu
- **80** 80 hachijyu
- **90** 90 kyujyu
- **100** 100 hyaku
- **101** 101 hyaku ichi
- **120** 120 hyaku nijyu
- **200** 200 nihyaku
- **500** 500 gohyaku
- **1000** 1000 sen
- **1 million** 100万 hyaku man
- **1 billion** 10億 jyu oku
- **1st** 1番 ichi ban
- **2nd** 2番 ni ban
- **3rd** 3番 san ban
- **4th** 4番 yon ban
- **5th** 5番 go ban
- **6th** 6番 roku ban
- **7th** 7番 nana ban / shichi ban
- **8th** 8番 hachi ban
- **9th** 9番 kyu ban
- **10th** 10番 jyu ban

BASICS

DAYS 日にち hinichi	**MONTHS** 月 tsuki

Monday
月曜日 getsuyobi

Tuesday
火曜日 kayobi

Wednesday
水曜日 suiyobi

Thursday
木曜日 mokuyobi

Friday
金曜日 kinyobi

Saturday
土曜日 doyobi

Sunday
日曜日 nichiyobi

public holidays
祝日 shukujitsu

weekdays
平日 heijitsu

weekends
週末 shumatsu

January
1月 ichi gatsu

February
2月 ni gatsu

March
3月 san gatsu

April
4月 shi gatsu

May
5月 go gatsu

June
6月 roku gatsu

July
7月 shichi gatsu

August
8月 hachi gatsu

September
9月 ku gatsu

October
10月 jyu gatsu

基本

November
11月 jyuichi gatsu

December
12月 jyuni gatsu

TIME
時間 jikan

in the morning
午前
gozen

in the afternoon
午後
gogo

in the evening
夕方
yugata

What is the time?
何時ですか?
nanji desuka?

twenty past two
2時20分です。
niji nijuppun desu

early
早い
hayai

late
遅い
osoi

it's quarter to three
3時15分前です
sanji jugo fun mae desu

it's one o'clock
1時です。
ichiji desu

it's half past two
2時半です。
nijihan desu

at 10 a.m. (10:00)
午前10時です。
gozen juji desu

at 9 p.m. (21:00)
午後9時です。
gogo kuji desu

now
今 ima

the day after tomorrow
明後日
asatte

23

BASICS

the day before yesterday
一昨日 ototoi

this morning
今朝
kesa

yesterday evening
昨晩
sakuban

tomorrow morning
明日の朝
asuno asa

this week
今週
konshu

next week
来週
raishu

What is today's date?
今日は何日ですか？
kyowa nannichi desuka

It's 13 September
9月13日です。
kugatsu jusan nichi desu

GREETINGS
挨拶
aisatsu

Good morning
おはよう ohayo

Good afternoon
こんにちは konnichiwa

Good evening
こんばんは konbanwa

Good night
おやすみ oyasumi

Hello
こんにちは konnichiwa

Goodbye
さよなら sayonara

See you soon
では、また
dewa mata

See you later
では、あとで
dewa atode

Cheerio
バイバイ bai bai

基本

Have a good time
楽しんでください。
tanoshinde kudasai

I have to go now
急いでいます。
isoide imasu

It was very nice
すごくよかったです。
sugoku yokatta desu

My name is ...
私の名前は...です。
watashino namae wa ... desu

What is your name?
あなたのお名前は何ですか?
anata no onamae wa nandesuka?

Pleased to meet you!
はじめまして!
hajimemashite!

How are you?
元気ですか?
genki desuka?

Fine, thanks. And you?
元気です。あなたは?
genki desu anatawa?

GENERAL
一般 ippan

Do you speak English?
英語を話しますか?
eigo wo hanashi masuka?

I don't understand
わかりません。
wakarimasen

Please speak slowly
ゆっくり話してください。
yukkuri hanashite kudasai

Please repeat that
もう一度お願いします。
moichido onegai shimasu

Please write it down
書いてください。
kaite kudasai

Excuse me please
すみません sumimasen

Could you help me?
手伝ってくれますか?
tetsudatte moraemasuka

Could you do me a favour?
お願いがあるのですが?
onegaiga aruno desuga?

25

BASICS

Can you show me?
見せてください。
misete kudasai?

how?
どうやるのですか?
dou yaruno desuka?

where?
どこですか?
doko desuka?

when?
いつですか?
itsu desuka?

who?
誰ですか?
dare desuka?

why?
なぜですか?
naze desuka?

which?
どちらですか?
dochira desuka?

I need ...
...が必要です。
...ga hitsuyo desu

yes, no
はい、いいえ
hai, iie

FORMS AND SIGNS
用紙とサイン
yoshi to sain

Please complete in block letters
ブロック体で記入してください。 burokku tai de kinyu shitekudasai

Surname
名字 myoji

First name(s)
名前 namae

Date of birth
生年月日 seinen gappi

Place of birth
出生地 shusseichi

Occupation
職業 shokugyo

Nationality
国籍 kokuseki

Address
住所
jyusho

基本

Date of arrival/ departure
到着日 / 出発日
touchakubi / shuppatsubi

Passport number
パスポート番号
pasupoto bango

I.D. number
ID番号
aidi bango

Issued at
...にて発行
...nite hakko

Engaged, Vacant
空きなし、空きあり
akinashi, akiari

No trespassing
進入禁止
shinnyu kinshi

Out of order
故障中
koshochu

Push, Pull
押す, 引く
osu, hiku

Please don't disturb
起こさないで下さい
okosanaide kudasai

Lift/Elevator
エレベーター
erebeta

Escalator
エスカレーター
esukareta

Wet paint
ペンキ塗りたて

Open, Closed
開店、閉店
kaiten, heiten

Opening hours
営業時間
eigyojikan

Self-service
セルフサービス
serufu sabisu

Waiting Room
待合室
machiai shitsu

TRANSPORT

BUS/TRAM STOP 29
バス停 / 路面電車駅
basutei / romendensha eki

UNDERGROUND/SUBWAY/METRO 30
地下鉄 chikatetsu

TRAIN/RAILWAY 30
電車 densha

BOATS 32
ボート boto

TAXI 33
タクシー takushi

AIRPORT 34
空港 kuko

ROAD TRAVEL/CAR HIRE 36
ドライブ / レンタカー
doraibu / rentaka

ROAD SIGNS 38
標識
hyoshiki

交通

> **BUS/TRAM STOP**
> バス停 / 路面電車駅
> basutei / romendensha eki

Where is the bus/tram stop?
バス停 / 路面電車駅はどこですか？
basutei / romendenshaeki wa dokodesuka?

Which bus do I take?
どのバスに乗ればいいですか？ dono basu ni noreba iidesuka?

How often do the buses go?
バスは何分おきに出ますか？ basu wa nanfun okini demasuka?

When is the last bus?
最終バスは何時ですか？
saishu basu wa nanjidesuka?

Which ticket must I buy?
どの切符を買えばいいですか？
dono kippu wo kaeba iidesuka?

Where must I go?
どこに行けばいいですか？
dokoni ikeba iidesuka?

I want to go to ....
...に行きたいです。
...ni ikitaidesu

What is the fare to...?
...までは幾らですか？
...made wa ikuradesuka?

When is the next bus?
次のバスは何時ですか？
tsugino basu wa nanjidesuka?

TRANSPORT

UNDERGROUND/SUBWAY/METRO
地下鉄
chikatetsu

entrance, exit
入り口 / 出口
iriguchi / deguchi

inner zone, outer zone
市内、郊外
shinai, kogai

Where is the underground/subway station?
地下鉄の駅はどこですか？
chikatetsuno eki wa dokodesuka?

Do you have a map for the metro?
地下鉄の地図はありますか？
chikatetsuno chizu wa arimasuka?

I want to go to ....
...に行きたいです。
...ni ikitaidesu

Can you give me change?
お釣りをください。？
otsuri wo kudasai?

Which ticket must I buy?
どの切符を買えばいいですか？ dono kippu wo kaeba idesuka?

When is the next train?
次の電車は何時ですか？
tsugino densha wa nanji desuka?

TRAIN/RAILWAY
電車
densha

Where is the railway station?
駅はどこですか？
eki wa dokodesuka?

交通

departure
出発
shuppatsu

arrival
到着
tochaku

Which platform?
何番線ですか？
nanbansen desuka?

Do you have a timetable?
時刻表はありますか？
jikokuhyo wa arimasuka?

A ... ticket please
...の切符をください。
...no kippu wo kudasai

- **single**
- 片道
  katamichi

- **return**
- 往復
  ofuku

- **child's**
- 子供
  kodomo

- **first class**
- 1等席 itto seki

- **second class**
- 2等席
  nito seki

- **smoking**
- 喫煙 kitsuen

- **non-smoking**
- 禁煙 kinen

Do I have to pay a supplement?
追加料金が必要ですか？
tsuika ryokin wa hitsuyo desuka?

Is my ticket valid on this train?
この切符は使えますか？
kono kippu wa tsukae-masuka?

TRANSPORT

Where do I have to get off?
どこで降りればいいですか?
dokode orireba iideuka?

I want to book ...
...を予約したいです。
...wo yoyaku shitaidesu

◆ **a seat**
◆ 席 seki

◆ **a couchette**
◆ 寝台車 shindaisha

Is this seat free?
この席は空いてますか?
konoseki wa aitemasuka?

That is my seat
私の席です。
watashino sekidesu

May I open (close) the window?
窓を開けて(閉めて)いいですか? mado wo akete (shimete) iidesuka?

Where is the restaurant car?
食堂車はどこですか?
shokudosha wa dokodesuka?

Is there a sleeper?
寝台はありますか?
shindai wa arimasuka?

EC – Eurocity
ユーロシティー
Eurocity

IC – Intercity
インターシティー
Intercity

stationmaster
駅長
ekicho

BOATS
ボート
boto

cruise
クルーズ
kuruzu

交通

Can we hire a boat?
ボートを貸してくれますか？ boto wo kashitekuremasuka?

How much is a round trip?
往復はいくらですか？ ofuku wa ikuradesuka?

one ticket
1枚
ichimai

two tickets
2枚
nimai

Can we eat on board?
中で食事ができますか？ nakade shokuji ga dekimasuka?

When is the last boat?
最終ボートは何時ですか？ saishu boto wa nanjidesuka?

When is the next ferry?
次のフェリーは何時ですか？ tsugino feri wa nanjidesuka?

How long does the crossing take?
何時間かかりますか？ nanjikan kakarimasuka?

Is the sea rough?
海は荒れてますか？ umi wa aretemasuka?

TAXI
タクシー
takushi

Please order me a taxi
タクシーを呼んでください。
takushi wo yondekudasai

Where can I get a taxi?
どこでタクシーに乗れますか？ dokode takushi ni noremasuka

TRANSPORT

To this address, please
この住所までお願いします。kono jusho made onegaishimasu

How much is it to the centre?
街までいくらですか？
machimade ikuradesuka?

To the airport, please
空港までお願いします。
kuko made onegaishimasu

To the station, please
駅までお願いします。
eki made onegaishimasu

Keep the change
おつりはいりません。
otsuri wa irimasen

I need a receipt
領収書をください。
ryoshusho wo kudasai

AIRPORT
空港
kuko

arrival
到着
tochaku

departure
出発
shuppatsu

flight number
フライト番号
furaito bango

delay
遅れ
okure

check-in
チェックイン
chekku in

hand luggage
手荷物
tenimotsu

交通

boarding card
搭乗券
tojo ken

gate
ゲート
geto

valid, invalid
有効、無効
yuko, muko

baggage/luggage claim
手荷物受取所
tenimotsu uketorijyo

lost property office
紛失物事務所
funshitsubutsu jimusho

Where do I get the bus to the centre?
街に行くバスはどれですか？
machini iku basu wa doredesuka?

Where do I check in for ...?
どこで...にチェックインできますか？ dokode...ni chekku in dekimasuka?

An aisle/window seat, please
通路側 / 窓側をお願いします。
tsurogawa / madogawa wo onegaishimasu

Where is the gate for the flight to ....?
...行きのゲートはどこですか？ ...ikino geto wa dokodesuka?

I have nothing to declare
申告するものはありません。 shinkoku surumono wa arimasen

It's for my own personal use
自分で使います。
jibun de tsukaimasu

TRANSPORT

The flight has been cancelled
飛行機がキャンセルされました。
hikoki ga kyanseru saremashita

The flight has been delayed
飛行機は遅れています。
hikoki wa okureteimasu

ROAD TRAVEL/ CAR HIRE
ドライブ / レンタカー
doraibu / rentaka

Have you got a road map?
道路地図はありますか？
dorochizu arimasuka?

How many kilometres is it to ...?
...まで何キロですか？
...made nan kiro desuka?

Where is the nearest garage?
一番近いガソリンスタンドはどこですか？ ichiban chikai gasorinsutando wa dokodesuka?

Fill it up, please
満タンお願いします。
mantan onegaishimasu

Please check the oil, water, battery, tyres
オイル、水、バッテリ-、タイヤをチェックしてください
oiru, mizu, batteri, taiya wo chekku shitekudasai

I'd like to hire a car
レンタカーを借りたいです。 rentaka wo karitai desu

How much does it cost per day/week?
1日/1週間いくらですか？
ichinichi / isshukan ikura desuka?

交通

What do you charge per kilometre?
1キロいくらですか？
ichi kiro ikura desuka?

Is mileage unlimited?
距離に制限はありますか？ kyorini seigen wa arimasuka?

Where can I pick up the car?
レンタカーはどこですか？
rentaka wa dokodesuka?

Where can I leave the car?
車はどこに返せばいいですか？ kuruma wa dokoni kaeseba iidesuka?

garage
ガソリンスタンド
gasorinsutando

headlight
ヘッドライト
heddo raito

windscreen
窓ガラス
mado garasu

indicator
方向指示器
hoko shijiki

What is the speed limit?
制限速度は何キロですか？
seigensokudo wa nan kiro desuka?

The keys are locked in the car
鍵を閉じ込めてしまいました。
kagi wo tojikomete shimaimashita

The engine is overheating
エンジンがオーバーヒートしました。
enjin ga ooba hiito shimashita

TRANSPORT

Have you got ...?
...を持ってますか？
...wo motte masuka?

◆ **a towing rope**
◆ 牽引ロープ
   kenin ropu

◆ **a spanner**
◆ スパナ
   supana

◆ **a screwdriver**
◆ スクリュードライバー
   sukuryu doraiba

ROAD SIGNS
標識
hyoshiki

No through road
行き止まり
ikidomari

one-way street
一方通行
ippo tsuko

entrance
入り口
iriguchi

exit
出口
deguchi

danger
危険
kiken

pedestrians
歩行者
hokosha

Keep entrance clear
入り口駐車禁止
iriguchi chusha kinshi

Residents only
住民のみ
jumin nomi

speed limit
制限速度
seigen sokudo

交通

stop
止まれ
tomare

No entry
進入禁止
shinnyu kinshi

roundabout
回り道
mawari michi

Insert coins
お金を入れてください。
okane wo irete kudasai

No Parking
駐車禁止
chusha kinshi

parking garage
駐車場
chushajyo

supervised car park
有人駐車場
yujin chushajyo

No right turn
右折禁止
usetsu kinshi

cul de sac
行き止まり
ikidomari

roadworks
工事中
koji chu

detour
回り道
mawari michi

Caution
注意
chui

uneven surface
でこぼこ道
dekoboko michi

toll
料金
ryokin

ACCOMMODATION

ACCOMMODATION 41
宿泊
shukuhaku

RECEPTION 43
受付
uketsuke

SELF-CATERING 44
自炊
jisui

CAMPING 46
キャンプ
kyampu

宿泊

ACCOMMODATION
宿泊 shukuhaku

hotel
ホテル hoteru

bed & breakfast
民宿 minshuku

vacancies
空室 kushitsu

Have you got a room ...?
いますか?
...heya ga aiteimasuka?

◆ **for tonight**
◆ 今夜 konya

◆ **with breakfast**
◆ 食付き choshoku tsuki

◆ **with bath**
◆ バス付 basu tsuki

◆ **with shower**
◆ シャワー付き
shawa tsuki

◆ **a single room**
◆ シングル部屋
shinguru beya

◆ **a double room**
◆ ダブル部屋
daburu beya

◆ **a family room**
◆ 家族部屋
kazokubeya

How much is the room per day/week?
一日/一週間 でいくらですか? ichinichi/isshukan de ikura desuka?

Have you anything cheaper/better?
もっと安い/もっと良い部屋ありますか?
motto yasui/motto yoi heya arimasuka?

Do you have a cot?
子供用ベットはありますか? kodomoyo beddo wa arimasuka?

ACCOMMODATION

What time is breakfast/dinner?
朝食/夕食は何時ですか？
choshoku / yushoku wa nanji desuka?

room service
ルームサービス
rumu sabisu

Please bring ...
... をお願いします。
...wo onegaishimasu

◆ **toilet paper**
◆ トイレットペーパー
　toiretto pepa

◆ **clean towels**
◆ きれいなタオル
　kireina taoru

Please clean the bath
浴室を掃除してください。
yokushitsu wo soji shite kudasai

Please put fresh sheets on the bed
ベットのシーツを換えてください。
beddo no shiitsu wo kaetekudasai

Please don't touch ...
...を触らないでください。
...sawaranaide kudasai

◆ **my briefcase**
◆ 私のブリーフケース
　watashi no burifu kesu

◆ **my laptop**
◆ 私のノートパソコン
　watashi no noto pasokon

My ... doesn't work
私の...が故障しています。watashino...ga kosho shiteimasu

◆ **toilet**
◆ トイレ toire

◆ **bedside lamp**
◆ ベットサイドランプ
　beddo saido rampu

宿泊

- ◆ air conditioning
- ◆ エアコン eakon

There is no hot water
お湯がでません。
oyu ga demasen

RECEPTION
受付 uketsuke

Are there any messages for me?
メッセージはありますか？
messeji (message) wa arimasuka?

Can I leave a message for someone?
メッセージを残したいのですが？ messeji wo nokoshitainodesuga?

Is there a laundry service?
クリーニングサービスはありますか？ kuriningu sabisu wa arimasuka?

Where is the lift/elevator?
エレベーターはどこですか？ erebeta wa dokodesuka?

Do you arrange tours?
観光の手配をしてくれますか？ kanko no tehai wo shitekuremasuka?

I need a wake-up call at 7 o'clock
7時にモーニングコールをお願いします。
shichiji ni moningu koru wo onegaishimasu

What number must I dial for room service?
ルームサービスは何番ですか？ rumu sabisu wa nanban desuka?

Please prepare the bill
お勘定お願いします。
okanjo onegai shimasu

There is a mistake in this bill
勘定があってません。
kanjo ga attemasen

ACCOMMODATION

I'm leaving tomorrow
明日、発ちます。
asu tachimasu

SELF-CATERING
自炊 jisui

Have you any vacancies?
空き部屋はありますか？
akibeya wa arimasuka?

How much is it per night/week?
一晩 / 一週間幾らですか？ hitoban / isshukan ikura desuka?

Do you allow
...を許可しますか？
...wo kyoka shimasuka

♦ **children**
♦ 子供 kodomo

Please, show me how ... works
...はどうやって使うのですか？ ...douyatte tsukauno desuka

♦ **the cooker / stove**
♦ クッカー / ストーブ
kukka / sutobu

♦ **the washing machine**
♦ 洗濯機 sentakuki

♦ **the dryer**
♦ ドライヤー doraiya

♦ **the heater**
♦ ヒーター hiita

♦ **the water heater**
♦ 湯沸かし器
yuwakashiki

Where is/are ...?
...はどこですか？
...wa dokodesuka

♦ **the switch**
♦ スイッチ suicchi

♦ **the fuses**
♦ ヒューズ hyuzu

Is there ...?
...はありますか？
...arimasuka

宿泊

- ◆ **a cot**
- ◆ 子供用ベッド
  kodomoyo beddo

- ◆ **a high chair**
- ◆ 子供用椅子
  kodomoyou isu

- ◆ **a safe**
  金庫 kinko

We need more ...
...をもっともらえますか？
...wo motto moraemasuka

- ◆ **cutlery**
- ◆ ナイフ、フォーク
  naifu, foku

- ◆ **crockery**
- ◆ 食器 shokki

- ◆ **sheets**
- ◆ シーツ
  shiitsu

- ◆ **blankets**
- ◆ 毛布
  mofu

- ◆ **pillows**
- ◆ 枕
  makura

Is there ... in the vicinity?
近くに...はありますか？
chikakuni...wa arimasuka

- ◆ **a shop**
- ◆ お店
  omise

- ◆ **a restaurant**
- ◆ レストラン
  resutoran

- ◆ **a bus/tram**
- ◆ バス/トラム
  basu / toramu

I have locked myself out
鍵を閉じ込めました。
kagi wo tojikomemashita

the keys
鍵
kagi

ACCOMMODATION

The window won't open/close
窓が 開きません/閉まりません。 mado ga akimasen / shimarimasen

CAMPING
キャンプ kyampu

caravan
キャラバン kyaraban

Have you got a list of camp sites?
キャンプ場のリストはありますか? kyampujo no risuto arimasuka?

Are there any sites available?
キャンプ場の空きはありますか? kyampujo no aki wa arimasuka?

Can we park the caravan here?
ここにキャラバンをとめていいですか?
kokoni kyaraban wo tomete iidesuka?

Can we camp here overnight?
ここでキャンプしていいですか?

kokode kyampu shite iidesuka?

This site is muddy
この場所はぬかってます。
konobasho wa nukattemasu

Is there a sheltered site?
屋根付きの場所はありますか?

yanetsuki no basho wa arimasuka?

Is there ... in the vicinity?
...は近くにありますか?
...wa chikakuni arimasuka?

◆ **a shop**
◆ お店 omise

◆ **a restaurant**
◆ レストラン resutoran

46

宿泊

Do you have electricity?
電気はありますか？
denki wa arimasuka?

We'd like to stay for three nights/a week
3日間/1週間泊まりたいです。mikkakan / isshukan tomaritai desu

Is there drinking water?
飲み水はありますか？
nomimizu wa arimasuka?

Can I light a fire here?
焚き火をしていいですか？
takibi wo shite iidesuka?

I'd like to buy fire wood
薪を買いたいです。
maki wo kaitaidesu

Is the wood dry?
薪は乾いていますか？
maki wa kawaite imasuka?

Do you have ... for rent?
...の貸し出しはありますか？ ...no kashidashi wa arimasuka?

- ◆ **a tent**
- ◆ テント
  tento

- ◆ **a gas cylinder**
- ◆ ガス
  gasu

- ◆ **a groundsheet**
- ◆ 防水シート
  bosui shiito

Where is/are the nearest ...?
近くに...はありますか？
chikakuni...arimasuka?

- ◆ **toilets**
- ◆ トイレ
  toire

- ◆ **sink (for dishes)**
- ◆ 流し
  nagashi

EATING AND DRINKING

CUTLERY 49
ナイフ、フォーク、スプーン
naifu, foku, supun

BREAKFAST 49
朝食 choshoku

LUNCH/DINNER 50
昼食 / 夕食 chushoku / yushoku

DRINKS 52
飲み物 nomimono

FOOD 53
食べ物 tabemono

DESSERTS AND CAKES 57
デザート、ケーキ
dezaato to keeki

飲食

CUTLERY
ナイフ、フォーク、スプーン
naifu, foku, supun

fork, cake fork
フォーク、ケーキ用フォーク foku, kekiyo foku

spoon, teaspoon
スプーン、ティースプーン
supun, ti supun

crockery
食器 shokki

plate
皿 sara

cup and saucer, mug
カップとソーサー、マグカップ kappu to sosa, magu kappu

BREAKFAST
朝食 choshoku

coffee
コーヒー kofi

- **with milk, cream**
- ミルク入り、クリーム入り miruku iri, kuriimu iri

- **black**
- ブラック burakku

- **without sugar**
- 砂糖なし satonashi

tea
紅茶 kocha

- **with milk, lemon**
- ミルク入り、レモン入り miruku iri, remon iri

bread
パン pan

rolls
ロールパン
rooru (roll) pan

egg(s)
卵 tamago

- **boiled – soft, hard**
- ゆでたまご－半熟、固め yude tamago - hanjuku, katame

- **fried**
- 目玉焼き
  medamayaki

49

EATING AND DRINKING

- ◆ **scrambled**
- ◆ スクランブル
  sukuranburu

- ◆ **poached**
- ◆ 落とし卵
  otoshi tamago

- ◆ **bacon and eggs**
- ◆ ベーコンと卵
  bekon to tamago

cereal
シリアル
shiriaru

hot milk, cold milk
暖かいミルク、冷たいミルク atatakai miruku, tsumetai miruku

fruit
果物
kudamono

orange juice
オレンジジュース
orenji jyusu

jam
ジャム
jamu

marmalade
マーマレード mamaredo

pepper
コショウ kosho

salt
塩 shio

> **LUNCH/DINNER**
> 昼食/夕食
> chushoku / yushoku

Could we have a table ...?
...の席はありますか？
...no seki wa arimasuka?

- ◆ **by the window**
- ◆ 窓際
  madogiwa

- ◆ **outside**
- ◆ 屋外 okugai

- ◆ **inside**
- ◆ 屋内 okunai

May I have ... ?
...をください。？
...kudasai?

飲食

- ◆ **the wine list**
- ◆ ワインリスト wain risuto

- ◆ **the menu of the day**
- ◆ 今日のお勧め kyono osusume

- ◆ **starters**
- ◆ 前菜 zensai

- ◆ **main course**
- ◆ メインコース mein koosu

- ◆ **dessert**
- ◆ デザート dezaato

What is this?
これは何ですか？
korewa nan desuka?

That is not what I ordered
これは、注文したものと違います。
korewa chumon shitamonoto chigaimasu

It's tough, cold, off
硬い、冷たい、痛んでいる
katai, tsumetai, itandeiru

What do you recommend?
お勧めは何ですか？
osusume wa nandesuka?

There is a mistake
間違いがありました。
machigai ga arimashita

Can I have the bill please?
勘定お願いします？
kanjo wo onegaishimasu?

We'd like to pay separately
別々に払います。
betsubetsu ni haraimasu

Thank you, that's for you
ありがとう。これはあなたに。
arigato korewa anatani

Keep the change
おつりはいりません。
otsuri wa irimasen

EATING AND DRINKING

DRINKS
飲み物
nomimono

a beer/lager – large, small
ビール / ラガー - 大、小
biru / raga – dai, sho

glass (¼ litre) of cider
サイダー (250ミリリットル) 一杯
saida nihyakugojyu miririttoru ippai

a dry white wine
ドライ白ワイン
dorai shiro wain

a sweet white wine
スウィート白ワイン
suito shiro wain

a light red wine
軽い赤ワイン
karui aka wain

house wine
ハウスワイン
hausu wain

a glass of wine with soda water
グラスワインのソーダ割り
gurasu wain no soda wari

champagne
シャンペン shanpen

a brandy
ブランデー burande

a whisky with ice
ウイスキー・ロック
uisuki rokku

liqueur
リキュール rikyuru

a glass
グラス gurasu

a bottle
ボトル
botoru

a mineral water – still, sparkling
ミネラルウォーター、スパークリングウォーター
mineraru wota, supakuringu wota

52

飲食

tap water
水道水 suidosui

fruit juice
フルーツジュース
furutsu jyusu

cola and lemonade
コーラとレモネード
kora to remonedo

another ... please
…もう一杯ください。
…mo ippai kudasai

too cold
冷えすぎです。
hiesugidesu

not cold enough
冷えていません。
hieteimasen

FOOD
食べ物
tabemono

Soup
スープ supu

pea, bean, lentil soup
豆スープ mame supu

Fish
魚 sakana

sole
カレイ karei

red mullet
赤ボラ aka bora

cod
タラ tara

perch
スズキ suzuki

salmon
鮭 sake

herring
ニシン nishin

trout
鱒 masu

blackfish
黒魚 kuro zakana

tuna
マグロ maguro

sardines
いわし iwashi

EATING AND DRINKING

fried, grilled, sautéed
揚げる、焼く、炒める
ageru, yaku, itameru

POULTRY
鳥 tori

chicken
鶏 niwatori

crumbed roasted chicken
ローストチキン
rosuto chikin

duck
カモ kamo

goose
ガチョウ gacho

roasted
ロースト rosuto

MEAT
肉 niku

mutton, lamb
羊、子羊 hitsuji, kohitsuji

beef
牛肉 gyuniku

veal
子牛の肉 koushinoniku

pork
豚肉 butaniku

sausage
ソーセージ soseji

veal sausage
子牛のソーセージ
koushi no soseji

venison
鹿肉 shikaniku

meat balls/cakes
ミートボール / ケーキ
mito boru / keeki

well done, medium, rare
ウェルダン、ミディアム、レアー
werudan, midiamu, rea

boiled, stewed
ゆで、シチュー
yude, shichu

smoked meats
燻製肉 kunsei niku

54

飲食

platter of cold meats
ハム類の盛り合わせ
hamurui no moriawase

PASTA AND RICE
パスタとご飯
pasuta to gohan

pasta made with cottage cheese
コテージチーズ入りのパスタ
koteji chizu irino pasuta

pasta with tomato sauce
トマトソースのパスタ
tomato sosu no pasuta

rice
ご飯 gohan

VEGETABLES, SALAD AND FRUIT
野菜、サラダ、果物
yasai, sarada, kudamono

eggplant
なす nasu

onion
たまねぎ tamanegi

cabbage
キャベツ kyabetsu

cauliflower
カリフラワー karifurawa

carrots
にんじん ninjin

green beans
インゲン豆 ingen mame

leeks
ねぎ negi

asparagus
アスパラガス
asuparagasu

peppers
ピーマン piman

pumpkin
かぼちゃ kabocha

lettuce
レタス retasu

beetroot
ビートルート
bitoruto

EATING AND DRINKING

cucumber
キュウリ kyuri

potatoes – boiled, fried, mashed
ジャガイモ – 茹でる、揚げる、マッシュ jagaimo – yuderu, ageru, masshu

root celery
セロリ serori

lemon
レモン remon

grapefruit
グレープフルーツ gurepu furutsu

apples
りんご ringo

pears
梨 nashi

bananas
バナナ banana

pineapple
パイナップル painappuru

cherries
さくらんぼ sakuranbo

strawberries
イチゴ ichigo

apricots
アプリコット apurikoto

peaches
桃 momo

raspberries
ラズベリー razuberi

blackberries
ブラックベリー burakkuberi

plums
プラム puramu

prunes
プルーン purun

grapes
ブドウ budo

dried fruit
ドライフルーツ dorai furutsu

飲食

cranberries
クランベリー
kuranberi

> **DESSERTS AND CAKES**
> デザートとケーキ
> dezaato to keeki

fruit salad
フルーツサラダ
furutsu sarada

jelly
ゼリー zeri

crème caramel
カスタードプリン
kasutado purin

meringue
メレンゲ merenge

pastry with apples and raisins
リンゴと干しブドウの菓子パン ringo to hoshibudo no kashipan

light fruitcake
軽いフルーツケーキ
karui furutsu keeki

baklava
バクラバ
bakuraba

fruit flan
フルーツフラン
furutsu furan

kataifi
カタイフィ
kataifi

custard pie
カスタードパイ
kasutado pai

chocolate cream cake
チョコレートクリームケーキ
chokoreto kurimu keki

vanilla cream cake
バニラクリームケーキ
banira kurimu keki

biscuits
ビスケット
bisuketo

MONEY AND SHOPPING

MONEY 59
お金 okane

POST OFFICE 60
郵便局 yubinkyoku

SHOPPING 60
買い物 kaimono

BUYING FOOD 62
食料購入 shokuryo konyu

BUYING CLOTHES 64
衣服購入 ifuku konyu

CLOTHING SIZES 65
服のサイズ fuku no saizu

お金と買い物

MONEY
お金
okane

bureau de change
両替所
ryogaejo

cash dispenser/ATM
ATM
ATM

Where can I change money?
どこで両替できますか？
dokode ryogae dekimasuka

Where is an ATM, a bank?
ATM、銀行はどこですか？
ATM, ginko wa dokodesuka?

When does the bank open/close?
銀行は何時に開きますか/ 閉まりますか？
ginko wa nanji ni akimasuka / shimarimasuka?

How much commission do you charge?
手数料はいくらですか？
tesuryo wa ikuradesuka?

I want to …
…したいです。
…shitai desu

◆ **cash a traveller's cheque**
◆ トラベラーズチェックを現金に toraberazu chekku wo genkin ni

◆ **change £50**
◆ 50ポンドを両替
goju pondo wo ryogae

MONEY AND SHOPPING

- ◆ **make a transfer**
- ◆ 振込み
  furikomi

> **POST OFFICE**
> 郵便局
> yubinkyoku

How much is ...?
...幾らですか？
...ikura desuka

- ◆ **a letter**
- ◆ 手紙
  tegami

- ◆ **a postcard to ...**
- ◆ はがき
  hagaki

- ◆ **a small parcel**
- ◆ 小包
  kozutsumi

Where can I buy stamps?
どこで切手を買えますか？
dokode kitte wo kaemasuka?

> **SHOPPING**
> 買い物
> kaimono

What does it cost?
幾らですか？
ikura desuka?

How much is it (total)?
(合計)幾らですか？
(goukei) ikuradesuka?

I need a receipt
レシートを下さい。
reshito wo kudasai

お金と買い物

Do you accept credit cards?
クレジットカードは使えますか?
kurejito cado wa tsukaemasuka

Do you take traveller's cheques?
トラベラーズチェックは使えますか?
toraberazu chekku wa tsukaemasuka?

Where do I pay?
どこで払いますか?
dokode harai masuka?

Does that include VAT?
税込みですか?
zei komi desuka?

Do you need a deposit?
前金が必要ですか?
maekin ga hitsuyo desuka?

Can you wrap it up for me?
これを包装してください。
kore wo hososhite kudasai

This isn't what I want
これはいりません。
korewa irimasen

This isn't correct (bill)
金額が違います。
kingaku ga chigaimasu

I want my money back
返金してください。
henkin shite kudasai

MONEY AND SHOPPING

This is ...
これは...
korewa...

- **broken**
- 壊れています。
  kowarete imasu

- **damaged**
- 傷んでいます。
  itande imasu

Can you repair it?
修理できますか？
shuri dekimasuka?

BUYING FOOD
食料購入
shokuryo konyu

Where can I buy ...?
どこで...を買えますか？
dokode... kaemasuka?

- **bread**
- パン
  pan

- **cake**
- ケーキ
  keki

- **cheese**
- チーズ
  chizu

- **butter**
- バター
  bata

- **milk**
- 牛乳
  gyunyu

- **water**
- 水
  mizu

- **wine**
- ワイン wain

- **sparkling wine**
- スパークリングワイン
  supakuringu wain

お金と買い物

- **beer**
- ビール
  biru

- **fruit juice**
- フルーツジュース
  furutsu jusu

- **meat**
- 肉
  niku

- **ham**
- ハム
  hamu

- **polony/cold meats**
- ソーセージ / ハム類
  soseji / hamurui

- **vegetables**
- 野菜 yasai

- **fruit**
- フルーツ furutsu

- **eggs**
- 卵
  tamago

I'll take ...
...を下さい。
...kudasai

- **one kilo**
- 1キロ
  ichi kiro

- **three slices**
- 3枚
  san mai

- **a portion of**
- 一塊
  hito katamari

- **a packet of**
- 1パック
  ichi pakku

- **a dozen**
- 1ダース ichi daasu

63

MONEY AND SHOPPING

BUYING CLOTHES
衣服購入
ifuku konyu

Can I try this on?
試着していいですか？
shichakushite iidesuka?

It is ...
これは...
korewa...

- **too big**
- 大きすぎです。
  okisugi desu

- **too small**
- 小さすぎです。
  chisasugi desu

- **too tight**
- きつすぎです。
  kitsusugi desu

- **too wide**
- ゆるすぎです。
  yurusugi desu

- **too expensive**
- 高すぎです。
  takasugi desu

I'll take ...
...を下さい。
...kudasai

- **this one**
- これ
  kore

- **size 40**
- サイズ40
  saizu 40

- **two**
- 2
  ni

お金と買い物

CLOTHING SIZES 服のサイズ
fuku no saizu

Women's Wear

UK	Asia	USA
10	M (28–30)	8
12	L (32–34)	10
14	XL (34–36)	12
16	XXL (36–38)	14
18	XXXL (38–40)	16

Menswear

UK	Asia	USA
36	S (26–28)	36
38	M (28–30)	38
40	L (32–34)	40
42	XL (34–36)	42
44	XXL (36–38)	44
46	XXXL (38–40)	46

Men's Shirts

UK	Asia	USA
14	S	14
14.5	M	14.5
15	L	15
15.5	XL	15.5
16	XXL	16
17	XXXL	17

Shoes

UK	Asia	USA
5	38 (F), 39 (M)	6
6	39 (F), 40 (M)	7
7	40 (F), 41 (M)	8
8	41 (F), 41 (M)	9
9	42 (F), 43 (M)	10
10	43 (F), 44 (M)	11
11	44 (F), 45 (M)	12

ACTIVITIES

SIGHTSEEING 67
観光
kanko

ENTERTAINMENT 68
エンターテイメント
entateimento

SPORT 69
スポーツ
supotsu

アクティビティ

SIGHTSEEING
観光 kanko

tourist office
観光案内所
kanko annaijo

Do you have leaflets?
パンフレットありますか？
panfuretto arimasuka?

I/We want to visit ...
...に行きたいです。
...ni ikitaidesu

When is it open/closed?
何時に開きますか？閉まりますか？
nanji ni akimasuka / shimarimasuka?

What does it cost?
いくらですか？
ikuradesuka?

Are there any reductions for ...?
...割引ありますか？
...waribiki arimasuka?

- **children**
- 子供
  kodomo

- **senior citizens**
- シニア
  shinia

- **students**
- 学生
  gakusei

Are there any tours?
どんな観光がありますか？ donna kanko ga arimasuka?

When does the bus depart/return?
バスは何時に出ますか？戻りますか？
basu wa nanji ni demasuka / modori masuka?

From where does the bus leave?
バスはどこから出ますか？
basu wa dokokara demasuka?

ACTIVITIES

Where is the museum?
博物館はどこですか?
hakubutsukan wa dokodesuka?

ENTERTAINMENT
エンターテイメント
entateimento

Is there a list of cultural events?
カルチャーイベントのリストはありますか?
karucha ibento no risuto wa arimasuka?

Are there any festivals?
フェスティバルはありますか?
fesutibaru wa arimasuka?

I'd like to go to ...
...に行きたいです。
...ni ikitaidesu

- **the theatre**
- シアター shiata

- **the opera**
- オペラ opera

- **the ballet**
- バレエ baree

- **the cinema/movies**
- 映画館 eigakan

- **a concert**
- コンサート konsato

Do I have to book?
予約が必要ですか?
yoyaku ga hitsuyo desuka?

How much are the tickets?
チケットはいくらですか?
chiketto wa ikura desuka?

Two tickets for ...
...のチケットを2枚ください。
...no chiketto wo nimai kudasai

- **tonight**
- 今夜 konya

- **tomorrow night**
- 明日の夜 asu no yoru

アクティビティ

- **the late show**
- 最後の上映
  saigo no joei

When does the performance start/end?
何時にはじまりますか？
終わりますか？
nanji ni hajimarimasuka /
nanjini owarimasuka?

Where is ...?
...はどこですか？
...wa dokodesuka?

- **a good bar**
- 良いバー yoi ba

- **good live music**
- 良いライブミュージック
  yoi raibu myu-jikku

Is it expensive?
高いですか？
takai desuka?

Is it noisy, crowded?
うるさいです、混んでいます。? urusaidesu,
kondeimasu?

SPORT
スポーツ supotsu

Where can we ...?
どこで...できますか？
dokode...dekimasuka?

- **go skiing**
- スキー suki

- **play tennis/golf**
- テニス / ゴルフ
  tenisu / gorufu

- **go swimming**
- 水泳 suiei

- **go fishing**
- 釣り tsuri

- **go riding**
- 乗馬 joba

- **go cycling**
- サイクリング
  saikuringu

- **hire bicycles**
- 自転車レンタル
  jitensha rentaru

ACTIVITIES

- **hire golf clubs**
- ゴルフクラブレンタル gorufu kurabu rentaru

- **hire skis**
- スキーレンタル suki rentaru

- **hire a boat**
- ボートレンタル boto rentaru

How much is it ...?
...いくらですか？ ...ikuradesuka?

- **per hour**
- 1時間 ichi jikan

- **per day**
- 1日 ichi nichi

- **per session/game**
- 1ゲーム ichi gemu

Is it ...?
...ですか？ ...desuka?

- **deep**
- 深い fukai

- **clean**
- きれい kirei

- **cold**
- 冷たい tsumetai

How do we get there?
どうやってそこに行きますか？

douyatte sokoni ikimasuka?

No swimming/diving
水泳禁止 / 飛び込み禁止 suiei kinshi / tobikomi kinshi

Are there currents?
流れは強いですか？
nagare wa tsuyoi desuka?

Do I need a fishing permit?
釣りの許可が必要ですか？ tsuri no kyoka ga hitsuyo desuka?

Where can I get one?
どこで許可が取れますか？ dokode kyoka ga toremasuka?

アクティビティ

Is there a guide for walks?
ウオーキングガイドがいますか? uookingu gaido ga imasuka?

Do I need walking boots?
ウオーキングブーツが必要ですか?
uookinngu buutsu ga hitsuyo desuka?

How much is a ski pass?
スキーパスはいくらですか? suki pasu wa ikura desuka?

Is it safe to ski today?
今日、スキーは安全ですか? kyo suki wa anzen desuka?

Run closed
コース閉鎖 kosu heisa

avalanches
なだれ nadare

I'm a beginner
初心者 shoshinsha

Danger
危険 kiken

Which is an easy run?
どちらが簡単ですか?
dochiraga kantan desuka?

My skis are too long/short
スキーの板が長すぎます / 短かすぎます。
suki no itaga nagasugimasu / mijikasugimasu

We want to go ...
...に行きたいです。
...ni ikitaidesu

- ◆ **hiking**
- ◆ ハイキング
   haikingu

- ◆ **sailing**
- ◆ セイリング seiringu

- ◆ **ice-skating**
- ◆ アイススケート
   aisu suketo

- ◆ **water-skiing**
- ◆ 水上スキー suijo suki

HEALTH AND SAFETY

PHARMACY/CHEMIST 73
薬局 yakkyoku

DOCTOR 74
医者 isha

HOSPITAL 74
病院 byoin

POLICE 75
警察 keisatsu

EMERGENCIES 75
緊急 kinkyu

FIRE DEPARTMENT 76
消防署 shoubousho

THE HUMAN BODY 77
人体 jintai

安全衛生

PHARMACY/ CHEMIST
薬局 yakkyoku

health shop
ヘルスショップ
herusushoppu

Have you got something for ...?
...の薬はありますか？
...no kusuri wa arimasuka?

- **diarrhoea**
- 下痢 geri

- **cold, flu**
- 風邪 kaze

- **headache**
- 頭痛 zutsu

- **a sore throat**
- 喉の痛み
  nodo no itami

- **stomachache**
- 胃痛 itsu

- **car sickness**
- 車酔い kurumayoi

I need ...
...を下さい。
...wo kudasai

- **indigestion tablets**
- 消化不良の薬
  shokafuryo no kusuri

- **laxative**
- 下剤 gezai

- **sleeping tablets**
- 睡眠薬 suiminyaku

- **a painkiller**
- 痛み止め itamidome

Is it safe for children?
子供に安全ですか？
kodomoni anzen desuka?

I'm a diabetic
私は糖尿病患者です。
watashi wa tonyobyo kanja desu

I have high blood pressure
私は高血圧です。
watashi wa koketsuatsu desu

HEALTH AND SAFETY

I'm allergic to ...
...のアレルギーがあります。 ...no arerugi ga arimasu

DOCTOR
医者 isha

I am ill
私は病気です。
watashi wa byoki desu

I need a doctor
医者が必要です。
isha ga hitsuyodesu

He/she has a high temperature
彼 / 彼女は高熱があります。 kare / kanojo wa konetsu ga arimasu

It hurts
痛みます。 itamimasu

I am going to be sick!
具合が悪いです。
guai ga waruidesu

dentist
歯医者 haisha

I have toothache
歯が痛いです。
ha ga itaidesu

Optometrist
眼医者 meisha

HOSPITAL
病院 byoin

Will I have to go to hospital?
病院に行かないといけませんか？ byoin ni ikanaito ikemasenka?

Where is the hospital?
病院はどこですか？
byoin wa dokodesuka?

Which ward?
どの病棟ですか？
dono byoren desuka?

When are visiting hours?
面会時間はいつですか？
menkaijikan wa itsudesuka?

Where is casualty?
負傷者はどこですか？
fushosha wa dokodesuka

安全衛生

POLICE
警察 keisatsu

Call the police
警察を呼んでください。
keisatsu wo yondekudasai

I have been robbed
強盗にあいました。
goto ni aimashita

My car has been stolen
車が盗まれました。
kuruma ga nusumare-mashita

My car has been broken into
車上荒しにあいました。
shajoarashi ni aimashita

I want to report a theft
盗難届けを出したいです。
tonan todoke wo dashitai desu

I have been attacked
襲われました。
osowaremashita

I have been raped
強姦されました。
gokan saremashita

Where is the police station?
警察署はどこですか？
keisatsusho wa dokodesuka

EMERGENCIES
緊急 kinkyu

Call an ambulance
救急車を呼んでください。
kyukyusha wo yondekudasai

There's been an accident
事故がありました。
jiko ga arimashita

Someone is injured
誰か怪我をしています。
dareka kega wo shitei-masu

Hurry up!
急いでください！
isoide kudasai!

Could you please help me?
助けてくれますか？
tasuketekuremasuka?

Help!
助けて！ tasukete!

HEALTH AND SAFETY

This is an emergency!
緊急です！
kinkyudesu!

My son/daughter is missing
息子 / 娘が行方不明です。 musuko / musume ga yukuefumei desu

I need a report for my insurance
保険のために報告書が必要です。 hoken no tameni hokokusho ga hitsuyodesu

I want to phone my embassy
大使館に電話をしたいです。 taishikan ni denwa wo shitaidesu

I am lost
道に迷いました。
michi ni mayoimashita

He/she is ill
彼 / 彼女は病気です。
kare / kanojo wa byoki desu

FIRE DEPARTMENT
消防署 shoubousho

Fire!
火事！ kaji!

Look out!
気をつけて！
ki wo tsukete!

Call the fire department
消防車を呼んでください。
shoubousha wo yondekudasai

It's an electrical fire
漏電による火事です。
roden niyoru kaji desu

The address is ...
住所は...です。
jusho wa ...desu

I need ...
...が必要です。
...ga hitsuyoudesu

- ◆ **a fire extinguisher**
- ◆ 消火器 shokaki

- ◆ **medical assistance**
- ◆ 医療アシスタント
  iryo asisutanto

安全衛生

THE HUMAN BODY
人体 jintai

- brain 脳 no
- head 頭 atama
- hair 髪 kami
- ear 耳 mimi
- cheek 頬 hoho
- neck 首 kubi
- shoulder 肩 kata
- chest 胸 mune
- arm 腕 ude
- elbow 肘 hiji
- abdomen 腹部 fukubu
- hand 手 te
- thumb 親指 oyayubi
- finger 指 yubi
- nail 爪 tsume
- bone 骨 hone
- knee 膝 hiza
- shin bone 脛骨 sunebone
- ankle 足首 ashikubi
- foot 足 ashi
- toe つま先 tsumasaki

- forehead 額 hitai
- eyebrow 眉毛 mayuge
- eyelash 睫毛 matsuge
- eye 目 me
- face 顔 kao
- nose 鼻 hana
- lip 唇 kuchibiru
- mouth 口 kuchi
- tooth 歯 ha
- chin 顎 ago
- lung 肺 hai
- heart 心臓 shinzo
- stomach 胃 i
- liver 肝臓 kanzo
- intestines 腸 cho
- leg 足 ashi
- skin 皮膚 hifu
- heel 踵 kakato

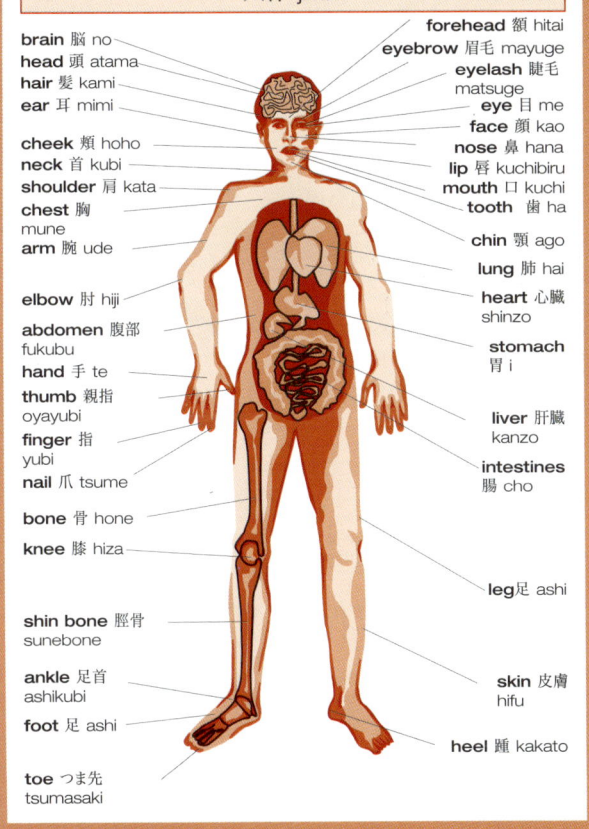

ETIQUETTE

FORMS OF ADDRESS 79
名前の呼び方 namae no yobikata

GREETINGS 79
あいさつ aisatsu

VISITING 80
訪問 homon

EATING 80
食事 shokuji

DRINKING 81
お酒 osake

BATHING 81
お風呂 ofuro

エチケット

FORMS OF ADDRESS

In Japan a person's first name follows their surname. It is common to address people by their last name. Only close friends and children are addressed by first name. People also usually attach a title to the name, depending on the social position of the person they are addressing. San is the most neutral title and can be used in most situations, whereas sama is more polite and is used in formal situations and letters.

GREETINGS

When greeting someone for the first time Japanese people say Hajime-mashite (it means 'it is first time'). In Japan people also greet each other by bowing. When bowing to someone of higher status a deeper bow indicates respect. In more casual settings a head nod is sufficient. If you are visiting on business exchanging business cards is a must in formal introductions. You should extend your card to the other person with both hands, and receive cards with both hands. Be sure to look at the card carefully to show respect and do not just pocket it. Never put it in your pants pocket.

ETIQUETTE

VISITING

If you are invited to someone's home it is polite to bring a small gift. Remember that when entering a Japanese house shoes are always removed. They are replaced by slippers, called genkan, which are provided by the host at the entrance. When entering a room with a tatami floor (mats woven from straw) it is customary to remove your slippers as well, and enter with bare feet or socks. Often there are special slippers to be worn to the toilet, and you may have to change your slippers before entering.

EATING

When dining out most restaurants will provide a hot towel for you to clean your hands before eating. It is generally considered impolite to wipe your face or neck. Before eating it is customary to say itadakimasu (it means 'allow me to have'). It is common for a table to share several bowls of food, so when moving food from shared plates onto your own you should use the opposite end of your chopsticks. Chopsticks should never be waved around, or used to spear food or point at anything, and you should never stick chopsticks into a bowl of rice. This is only done at funerals. If you cannot use chopsticks it is not considered bad manners to ask for a knife

エチケット

and fork, although some restaurants may not have them. When eating foods like soba or ramen noodles it is okay to slurp. It is, however, bad manners to blow your nose at the table. Outside of restaurants it is not common for people to eat and drink while walking, and some consider it rude to eat in public places.

DRINKING
When drinking it is customary to fill your companions' cups rather than serving yourself. Check occasionally to see whether your friends' cups are getting empty, and if so you should refill them. If someone offers to refill your cup, drain it before holding it out for a refill. You should not start drinking until everybody at the table has been served, when a toast is made by saying kampai (it means bottoms up).

BATHING
Bathing is important to the Japanese, as cleanliness is an essential aspect of the culture. Traditional Japanese baths are square, and the water is deep enough to cover the shoulders. Before bathing you will need to wash yourself and your hair, and ensure that all the soap is removed before getting into the bath tub. The reason for this is that the water is to be used not only by one person but the entire family.

HOLIDAYS AND FESTIVALS

NATIONAL HOLIDAYS 83
祝日
shukujitsu

FESTIVALS 84
祭り
matsuri

祝日と祭り

NATIONAL HOLIDAYS
祝日
shukujitsu

New Year's Day
(1 January)
New Year's Day has been a national holiday since 1948. It is the beginning of the New Year season which lasts for the first week of the year, and during which many businesses are closed.

National Foundation Day (11 February)
This holiday was established in 1966 as a day to celebrate the founding of the nation by Emperor Jimmu according to the 'Koji-Ki' and 'Nihon-Shoki'. It is now more focussed on nationalism than imperialism.

Constitution Day
(3 May)
This holiday commemorates the day the new constitution came into effect after World War II.

Greenery Day
(4 May)
This national holiday is celebrated as a day to commune with nature and be grateful for its blessings. This was originally held to celebrate the birthday of Emperor Shōwa on 29 April. Since the ascension of the new Emperor it has been renamed Showa Day, then move to 4 May, renamed Greenery Day. It falls during Golden Week, a week of Japanese holidays.

HOLIDAYS AND FESTIVALS

Children's Day
(5 May)
Children's Day marks the end of Golden Week. Traditionally a day for boys, families fly carp (khoi fish) kites from their houses. The symbol of carp swimming upstream represents sons growing strong.

Autumnal Equinox Day
(September)
This old traditional holiday honours the ancestors and the dead.

The Emperor's Birthday
(23 December)
The tradition of celebrating the reigning Emperor's birthday with a national holiday since 1868. Emperor Akihito, the current monarch, was born on this day in 1933.

> **FESTIVALS**
> 祭り
> matsuri

The Tondo Festival
(15 January)
Most communities hold a festival on this day to make bonfires from the old New Year's decorations. Children place examples of their calligraphy onto the fire, and if the smoke carries them away it means they will become good calligraphers. Traditional foods served on this day are pork stew and glutinous rice cakes, and sake is warmed in lengths of bamboo over the fire.

祝日と祭り

Beginning of Spring
Setsubun
(3 February)
This is not a national holiday but is celebrated across the country. A custom on this day is to throw beans around the house and at temples and shrines. Afterwards it is customary to pick up and eat a number of beans corresponding to your age.

The Star Festival
(7 July/7 August)
Known as Tanabata, this festival is celebrated on the seventh day of the seventh month of the year. In some parts of Japan this is on the 7th July and in others on the 7th August, depending on where the lunar calendar is used. The Star Festival celebrates the day on which two stars, Altair and Vega, meet according to Chinese legend. A custom on Tanabata is to write your wishes on a piece of paper, hang them on a special bamboo tree and wait for them to come true.

Chichibu Night Festival
(2–3 December)
This is one of Japan's most popular festivals and features a procession of huge, brightly lit and intricately decorated floats which parade through the city.

A

abbey 大修道院 dai shudoin
abortion 妊娠中絶 ninshin chuzetsu
about (approximately) 約 yaku
above 上 ue
abroad 海外 kaigai
abscess 膿瘍 noyou
absolutely 絶対に zettai ni
accelerator アクセル akuseru
accent アクセント akusento
accept 受け取る uketoru
accident 事故 jiko
accommodation 宿泊 shukuhaku
account 口座 koza
accurate 正確な seikakuna
ache 痛み itami
adapter アダプター adaputa
adhesive tape 接着テープ secchaku teipu
admission fee 入場料 nyujyoryo
adult 大人 otona
advance, in advance 前払い maebarai
advertisement 広告 kokoku
advice アドバイス adobaisu
advise アドバイスする adobaisu suru
aeroplane 飛行機 hikoki
afraid, be afraid of 怖い kowai
after 後 ato
afternoon 午後 gogo
afterwards 後で atode

again また mata
against 反対に hantai ni
age 年 toshi
agree 賛成 sansei
agreement 同意 doi
air 空気 kuki
air conditioning エアコン eakon
air ticket 航空券 kokuken
airmail 航空便 kokubin
airport 空港 kuko
aisle 通路 tsuro
aisle seat 通路側の席 tsurogawa no seki
all right 大丈夫 daijobu
allow 許す yurusu
almond アーモンド aamondo
almost ほとんど hotondo
alone 独りで hitoride
already すでに sudeni
also ～もまた ...mo mata
although ～だけれども ...dakeredomo
altogether 全体で zentai de
always いつも itsumo
a.m. (before noon) 午前 gozen
am, I am ～です。私は～です。 ...desu. Watashi wa ... desu
amazing すごい sugoi
amber アンバー anba
ambulance 救急車 kyukyusha
among ～の間に ...no aida ni
amount 量 ryo

anaesthetic 麻酔 masui
ancient 古代の kodaino
and 〜と ...to
angry 怒って okotte
animal 動物 dobutsu
ankle 足首 ashikubi
anniversary 記念日 kinenbi
annoy 困らせる komaraseru
annual 毎年の maitoshi no
another もう一つ mohitotsu
answer (n) 返事 henji
answer (vb) 返事する henji suru
ant 蟻 ari
antacid 酸中和剤 sanchuwa zai
anybody 誰か dareka
anything 何でも nandemo
apartment アパート apato
apology 謝罪 shazai
appendicitis 盲腸炎 mocho en
appointment 約束 yakusoku
approximately おおよそ ooyoso
apron エプロン epuron
are 〜です。 ...desu
area 地域 chiiki
armchair アームチェア aamuchea
arrange 用意をする yoi suru
arrest 逮捕 taiho
arrival 到着 tochaku
arrive 到着する tochaku suru
art 芸術 geijutsu
artist 芸術家 geijutsuka
ask 尋ねる tazuneru

astonishing 驚くべき odorokubeki
at 〜に ...ni
attack (n) 攻撃 kogeki
attack (vb) 攻撃する kogeki suru
attic 屋根裏 yaneura
audience 観客 kankyaku
aunt 叔母 oba
auto-teller ATM ATM
autumn 秋 aki
available 利用できる riyo dekiru
avalanche 雪崩 nadare
avenue 大通り oodori
average 平均 heikin
avoid 避ける sakeru
awake 目が覚める mega sameru
away 遠くに tokuni
awful ひどい hidoi

B

baby food ベビーフード bebi fudo
back 背中 senaka
backache 腰痛 yotsu
backpack バックパック bakku pakku
bacon ベーコン bekon
bad 悪い warui
bag バッグ baggu
baggage 手荷物 tenimotsu
baggage reclaim 手荷物受取所 tenimotsu uketoriyo
bait 餌 esa
bakery パン屋 panya

balcony バルコニー
   barukoni
ballpoint pen ボールペン
   boru pen
Baltic Sea バルト海
   baruto kai
bandage 包帯 houtai
bar of chocolate
   板チョコ ita choko
barber's shop 床屋
   tokoya
bark ほえる hoeru
barn 納屋 naya
barrel 樽 taru
basement 地下室
   chikashitsu
basket バスケット basuketto
bath お風呂 ofuro
bathroom 浴室 yokushitsu
bay 湾 wan
bay leaf ベイリーフ beirifu
be 存在する sonzai suru
beach ビーチ bichi
bean 豆 mame
beard あごひげ agohige
beautiful 美しい utsukushii
beauty salon
   ビューティサロン byuti saron
because なぜなら
   nazenara
because of
   〜のために ...no tameni
bed ベッド beddo
bed & breakfast
   民宿 minshuku
bed linen シーツと枕カバー
   shitsu to makura kaba
bedspread
   ベッドカバー beddo kaba

bee 蜂 hachi
beef 牛肉 gyuniku
beer ビール biru
before 〜する前に
   ...surumaeni
beginner 初心者
   shoshinsha
behind 〜の後ろに
   ...no ushironi
Belgian ベルギー人
   berugii jin
Belgium ベルギー berugii
believe 信じる shinjiru
bell ベル beru
below 〜より下に
   ...yori shitani
belt ベルト beruto
bend 曲げる mageru
beside 〜のそばに
   ...no sobani
bet 賭け kake
better より良い yoriyoi
beyond 〜を越えて
   ...o koete
bicycle 自転車 jitensha
big 大きい okii
bill 勘定 kanjyo
bin ゴミ箱 gomibako
binoculars 双眼鏡
   sogankyo
bird 鳥 tori
birth 出生 shussei
birth certificate
   出生証明書
   shussei shomeisho
birthday 誕生日 tanjyobi
birthday card
   誕生日カード
   tanjyobi kado

birthday present
誕生日プレゼント
tanjyobi purezento
biscuit ビスケット bisuketto
bit 少し sukoshi
bite 噛む kamu
black 黒 kuro
blackcurrant
ブラックカレント
burakkukarento
blanket 毛布 mofu
bleach 漂白剤 hyohakuzai
bleed 出血 shukketsu
blind (n) 日よけ hiyoke
blind (adj) 盲目 momoku
blister 水膨れ mizubukure
block of flats アパート
apato
blocked 閉鎖 heisa
blood 血 chi
blood pressure 血圧
ketsuatsu
blouse ブラウス burausu
blow-dry
ドライヤーで髪を乾かす
doraiyaa de kami wo
kawakasu
blue 青 ao
blunt 切れ味の悪い
kireaji no warui
blusher 赤面 sekimen
boar イノシシ inoshishi
boarding card 搭乗券
tojyoken
boarding house 寄宿舎
kishuku sha
boat ボート boto
boat trip 船旅 funatabi
body 身体 karada

boil (n) ゆで yude
boil (vb) ゆでる yuderu
bone 骨 hone
bonnet (car) ボンネット
bonnetto
book 本 hon
bookshop 本屋 honya
boots ブーツ bootsu
border 国境 kokkyo
boring 退屈な taikutsuna
born 生まれつきの
umaretsukino
borrow 借りる kariru
both 両方 ryoho
bottle ボトル botoru
bottle opener 栓抜き
sen nuki
bottom (at the) 下 shita
bow tie 蝶ネクタイ
cho nekutai
bowl ボール boru
box 箱 hako
boy 少年 shonen
boyfriend ボーイフレンド
boi furendo
bra ブラジャー burajya
bracelet ブレスレット
buresuretto
brake ブレーキ bureki
brake fluid ブレーキ液
bureki eki
brake light ブレーキライト
bureki raito
branch (office) 支店
shiten
brand ブランド burando
brandy ブランデー burande
bread パン pan
break 壊れる kowareru

breakable 壊れやすい kowareyasui
breakdown (of car) 故障 kosho
breakdown van 故障したバン koshoshita ban
breakfast 朝食 choshoku
break-in 強盗 goto
breast 胸 mune
breathe 呼吸する kokyu suru
breeze そよ風 soyokaze
brewery 醸造所 jyozosho
brick レンガ renga
bride 新婦 shimpu
bridegroom 新郎 shinro
bridge 橋 hashi
briefcase ブリーフケース burifu kesu
bright まぶしい mabushii
bring 持ってくる motte kuru
bring in 持ち込 mochikomu
brochure パンフレット panfuretto
broken 壊れた kowareta
bronchitis 気管支炎 kikanshien
brooch ブローチ burochi
broom ほうき hoki
brother 兄弟 kyoudai
brother-in-law 義理の兄弟 giri no kyodai
brown 茶色 chairo
bruise あざ aza
brush ブラシ burashi
Brussels ブリュッセル buryusseru
bucket バケツ baketsu

buffet car 食堂車 shokudosha
buggy バギー bagi
build 建てる tateru
building 建物 tatemono
bulb (light) 電球 denkyu
bulb (plant) 球根 kyukon
bumper バンパー bampa
bun ロールパン roru pan
bunch 束 taba
bureau de change 両替所 ryogaejo
burglar 泥棒 dorobo
burglary 窃盗 setto
burn 焼く yaku
burst 破裂する haretsu suru
bus バス basu
bus stop バス停 basu tei
bush 藪 yabu
business ビジネス bijinesu
business trip 出張 shuccho
busy 忙しい isogashi
but しかし shikashi
butcher 肉屋 nikuya
butter バター bata
butterfly 蝶 cho
button ボタン botan
buy 買う kau
by ～によって ...ni yotte
bypass (road) バイパス baipasu

C
cab タクシー takushi
cabbage キャベツ kyabetsu
cabin キャビン kyabin
cable car ケーブルカー keburuka

cake ケーキ keeki
cake shop ケーキ屋 keeki ya
calculator 計算機 keisanki
calf 子牛 koushi
call (n) 電話 denwa
call (vb) 呼び出し yobidashi
calm 冷静 reisei
camp キャンプ kyanpu
camp site キャンプ場 kyanpu jyo
can 缶 kan
can opener 缶切り kankiri
Canada カナダ kanada
canal 運河 unga
cancel キャンセルする kyanseru suru
cancellation キャンセル kyanseru
cancer 癌 gan
candle ろうそく rosoku
candy 飴 ame
canoe カヌー kanu
cap 帽子 boshi
capital (city) 首都 shuto
capital (money) 資本金 shihonkin
car 車 kuruma
car ferry カーフェリー kaa feri
car hire レンタカー rentaka
car insurance 車両保険 sharyo hoken
car keys 車の鍵 kuruma no kagi
car parts 車の部品 kuruma no buhin
car wash 洗車 sensha

caravan キャラバン kyaraban
caravan site キャラバン場 kyaraban jyo
carburettor キャブレター kyabureta
card カード kado
cardboard ダンボール danboru
cardigan カーディガン kadigan
careful 注意深い chui bukai
caretaker 世話人 sewanin
carpenter 大工 daiku
carpet 絨毯 jyutan
carriage 客車 kyakusha
carrier bag 買い物袋 kaimono bukuro
carrot にんじん ninjin
carry 運ぶ hakobu
carry-cot 携帯ベビーベッド keitai bebiibeddo
carton カートン katon
case ケース kesu
cash 現金 genkin
cash desk レジ reji
cash dispenser ATM ATM
cash register レジ reji
cashier レジ係り reji gakari
cassette カセット kasetto
castle 城 shiro
casualty department 救急病棟 kyukyu byoren
cat 猫 neko
catch 捕まえる tsukamaeru
cathedral 大聖堂 daiseido
Catholic カトリック katorikku

cauliflower カリフラワー karifurawaa
cave 洞窟 dokutsu
CD player CDプレイヤー CD pureia
ceiling 天井 tenjyo
celery セロリ serori
cellar 地下室 chikashitsu
cemetery 墓地 bochi
Centigrade 摂氏 sesshi
centimetre センチ senchi
central heating セントラルヒーティング sentoraru hitingu
central locking セントラルロッキング sentoraru rokkingu
centre センター senta
century 世紀 seiki
certain 確か tashika
certainly 確かに tashikani
certificate 証明書 shomeisho
chair 椅子 isu
chair lift チェアリフト chea rifuto
chambermaid 客室係 kyakushitsu gakari
champagne シャンペン shampen
change (n) 小銭 kozeni
change (vb) 変化する henka suru
changing room 着替え室 kigaeshitsu
channel チャンネル channeru
chapel 礼拝堂 reihaidou
charcoal 炭 sumi

charge 料金 ryokin
charge card クレジットカード kurejitto kado
charter flight チャーターフライト chata furaito
cheap 安い yasui
cheap rate 安い値段 yasui nedan
cheaper もっと安い motto yasui
check チェックする chekku suru
check in チェックイン chekku in
cheek ほお hoo
Cheers! 乾杯 kampai
cheese チーズ chizu
chef シェフ shefu
chemist 薬局 yakkyoku
cheque 小切手 kogitte
cheque book 小切手帳 kogittecho
cheque card 小切手カード kogittekado
cherry さくらんぼ sakurambo
chess チェス chesu
chest 胸 mune
chest of drawers たんす tansu
chestnut 栗 kuri
chewing gum チューインガム chuin gamu
chicken 鶏 niwatori
chicken pox 水疱瘡 mizuboso

child 子供 kodomo
child car seat チャイルドシート chairudoshito
chimney 煙突 entotsu
chin 顎 ago
China 中国 chugoku
china 陶器 toki
chips ポテトチップス poteto chippusu
chives アサツキ asatsuki
chocolate(s) チョコレート chokoreto
choir 聖歌隊 seikatai
choose 選ぶ erabu
chop チョップ choppu
Christian name クリスチャンネーム kurisuchan nemu
Christmas クリスマス kurisumasu
Christmas Eve クリスマスイブ kurisumasu ibu
church 教会 kyokai
cider サイダー saida
cigar 葉巻 hamaki
cigarette タバコ tabako
cigarette lighter ライター raita
cinema 映画 eiga
circle 円 en
cistern タンク tanku
citizen 市民 shimin
city 市 shi
city centre 都心 toshin
class クラス kurasu
clean (vb) 掃除する soji suru
clean (adj) きれい kirei

cleaning solution 清浄液 senjoeki
cleansing lotion クレンジングローション kurenjingu roshon
clear クリア kuria
clever 賢い kashikoi
client 顧客 kokyaku
cliff 崖 gake
climate 気候 kiko
climb 登る noboru
cling film サランラップ saranrappu
clinic 病院 byoin
cloakroom 預かり所 azukarijyo
clock 時計 tokei
closed 閉店 heiten
cloth 布 nuno
clothes 服 fuku
clothes line 物干し用ロープ monohoshiyo ropu
clothes peg 洗濯ばさみ sentaku basami
clothing 衣類 irui
cloud 雲 kumo
clutch (car) クラッチ kuracchi
coach コーチ kochi
coal 石炭 sekitan
coast 海岸 kaigan
coastguard 海岸警備 kaigankeibi
coat コート koto
coat hanger ハンガー hanga
cockroach ゴキブリ gokiburi
cocoa ココア kokoa

coconut ココナッツ kokonattsu
cod タラ tara
code コード kodo
coffee コーヒー kohi
coil (contraceptive) コイル koiru
coil (rope) ロープを巻く ropu wo maku
coin コイン koin
Coke コーラ kora
colander 水切りボール mizukiri boru
cold 冷たい tsumetai
collapse 崩壊 hokai
collar 襟 eri
collarbone 鎖骨 sakotsu
colleague 同僚 doryo
collect 集める atsumeru
collect call コレクトコール korekuto koru
colour 色 iro
colour blind 色弱 shiki jaku
colour film カラー映像 kara eizo
comb (n) くし kushi
comb (vb) くしでとく kushi de toku
come 来る kuru
come back 戻ってくる modottekuru
come in 中に入る naka ni hairu
comedy コメディ komedi
comfortable 心地よい kokochi yoi
company 会社 kaisha

compartment 区画 kukaku
compass コンパス konpasu
complain 苦情をいう kujyo wo iu
complaint 苦情 kujyo
completely 完全に kanzen ni
composer 作曲家 sakkyokuka
compulsory 必修の hisshu no
computer コンピューター kompyuta
concert コンサート konsato
concession 譲歩 jyoho
concussion 脳震盪 noshinto
condition 条件 jyoken
condom コンドーム kondomu
conference 会議 kaigi
confirm 確認する kakunin suru
confirmation 確認 kakunin
confused 混乱した konranshita
Congratulations! おめでとう! omedeto!
connecting flight 乗継便 noritsugibin
connection (elec) 接続 setsuzoku
connection (phone) 接続 setsuzoku
conscious 意識 ishiki
constipated 便秘で bempi de
consulate 領事館 ryojikan

contact 連絡する renraku suru
contact lenses コンタクトレンズ kontakuto renzu
continue 継続する keizoku suru
contraceptive 避妊薬 hininyaku
contract 契約 keiyaku
convenient 便利 benri
cook (n) コック kokku
cook (vb) 料理 ryori
cooker クッカー kukka
cookie クッキー kukki
cooking utensils 調理器具 chorikigu
cool 涼しい suzushii
cool bag, cool box クーラーボックス kura bokkusu
copy コピー kopi
cork コルク kuruku
corkscrew コルク栓抜き koruku sennuki
corner 角 kado
correct 正す tadasu
corridor 廊下 roka
cost 料金 ryokin
cot 簡易ベッド kan i beddo
cotton 綿 men
cotton wool 脱脂綿 dasshi men
couch カウチ kauchi
couchette 寝台 shindai
cough (n) 咳 seki
cough (vb) 咳をする seki wo suru
cough mixture 咳止め sekidome
Could I? 〜していいですか? ...shite iidesuka?
couldn't できない。dekinai
counter カウンター kaunta
country 国 kuni
countryside 田舎 inaka
couple カップル kappuru
courier service 宅急便 takkyubin
course コース koosu
cousin いとこ itoko
cover charge カバーチャージ kaba chaji
cow 牛 ushi
crab カニ kani
craft 飛行機 hikoki
cramp 痙攣 keiren
crash 激突する gekitotsu suru
crash helmet 安全ヘルメット anzen herumetto
crazy 正気でない shoki de nai
cream クリーム kurimu
crèche 託児所 takujisho
credit card クレジットカード kurejitto kado
crime 犯罪 hanzai
crisps カリカリした karikari shita
crockery 食器 shokki
cross (n) クロス kurosu
cross (vb) 交差する kosa suru
crossing 横断歩道 oudanhodo

crossroads 交差点 kosaten
crossword puzzle クロスワード kurosu wado
crowd 群集 gunshu
crowded 混んでいる kondeiru
crown 王冠 okan
cruise クルーズする kuruzu suru
crutches 松葉杖 matsubazue
cry 泣く naku
cucumber キュウリ kyuri
cufflinks カフスボタン kafusu botan
cup コップ koppu
cupboard 戸棚 todana
curly 巻き毛の makige no
currency 通貨 tsuka
current 流れ nagare
curtain カーテン katen
cushion クッション kusshon
custard カスタード kasutado
custom 習慣 shukan
customer お客様 okyakusama
customs 通関 tsukan
cut 切る kiru
cutlery ナイフ、フォーク naifu (knife), foku (fork)
cycle 周期 shuki
cycle track 自転車用道路 jitensha yo doro
cyst 嚢胞 noho
cystitis 膀胱炎 bokoen
Czech Republic チェコ共和国 cheko kyowakoku

D
daily 毎日 mainichi
damage ダメージ dameji
damp 湿った shimetta
dance ダンス dansu
danger 危険 kiken
dangerous 危険な kikenna
dark 暗い kurai
date (appointment) 約束 yakusoku
date (fruit) デイト deito
date (of year) 日にち hinichi
date of birth 生年月日 seinengappi
daughter 娘 musume
daughter-in-law 義理の娘 giri no musume
dawn 夜明け yoake
day 日にち hinichi
dead 死亡した shiboshita
deaf 聴覚障害の chokaku shogai no
deal 取引 torihiki
dear 大切な taisetsuna
death 死亡 shibo
debts 借金 shakkin
decaffeinated カフェイン抜きの kafein nokino
December 12月 jyuni gatsu
decide 決める kimeru
decision 決定 kettei
deck chair デッキチェア dekki chea
deduct 〜を差し引く ...o sashihiku
deep 深い fukai

definitely 絶対に zettai ni
degree (measurement) 程度 teido
degree (qualification) 学位 gakui
delay 遅れる okureru
deliberately 故意に koini
delicious おいしい oishi
deliver 配達する haitatsu suru
delivery 配達 haitatsu
Denmark デンマーク denmaku
dental floss 糸ようじ ito yoji
dentist 歯医者 haisha
dentures 総入れ歯 so ireba
depart 出発する shupatsu suru
department 部署 busho
department store デパート depato
departure 出発 shuppatsu
departure lounge 出発ラウンジ shupatsu raunji
deposit 前金 maekin
describe 〜を表現する ...o hyogen suru
description 表現 hyogen
desert 砂漠 sabaku
desk 机 tsukue
dessert デザート dezaato
destination 目的地 mokutekichi
details 詳細 shosai
detergent 洗剤 senzai
detour 寄り道 yorimichi

develop 発展する haten suru
diabetic 糖尿病患者 tonobyo kanjya
dial ダイアル daiaru
dialling code ダイアリングコード daiaringu kodo
dialling tone 発信音 hasshin on
diamond ダイアモンド daiamondo
diaper オムツ omutsu
diarrhoea 下痢 geri
diary 日記 nikki
dice さいころ saikoro
dictionary 辞書 jisho
die 死亡する shibo suru
diesel ディーゼル dizeru
diet ダイエット daietto
difference 違い chigai
different 違う chigau
difficult 難しい muzukashii
dinghy 薄汚れて usu yogorete
dining room ダイニングルーム dainingu rumu
dinner 夕食 yushoku
direct 直接 chokusetsu
direction 方角 hogaku
dirty 汚れた yogoreta
disabled 体の不自由な karadano fujiyuna
disappear 消える kieru
disappointed がっかりする gakkari suru
disaster 災害 saigai

disconnected 切断された setsudan sareta
discount 割引 waribiki
discover 発見する hakken suru
disease 病気 byoki
dish 食器 shokki
dishtowel 食器用タオル shokkiyo taoru
dishwasher 食器洗い機 shokki araiki
disinfectant 消毒剤 shodokuzai
disk ディスク disuku
disposable diapers/nappies 使い捨てオムツ tsukaisute omutsu
distance 距離 kyori
district 地区 chiku
disturb 〜を妨げる ...samatageru
dive 飛び込む tobikomu
diving board 飛び込み台 tobikomidai
divorced 離婚している rikon shiteiru
DIY shop 日曜大工店 nichiyo daikuten
dizzy めまいがする memaiga suru
do する suru
doctor 医者 isha
document 書類 shorui
dog 犬 inu
doll 人形 ningyo
domestic 国内の kokunaino
door ドア doa
doorbell ドアベル doaberu

doorman ドアマン doaman
double ダブル daburu
double bed ダブルベッド daburu beddo
double room ダブルルーム daburu rumu
doughnut ドーナツ donatsu
downhill 下り坂 kudari zaka
downstairs 階下 kaika
dozen ダース daasu
drain 下水管 gesui kan
draught 原稿 genko
draught beer 生ビール nama biru
drawer 引き出し hikidashi
drawing 絵 e
dreadful 恐ろしい osoroshii
dress 衣服 ifuku
dressing (bandage) 包帯 hotai
dressing (salad) ドレッシング doreshingu
dressing gown ガウン gaun
drill ドリル doriru
drink (n) 飲み物 nomimono
drink (vb) 飲む nomu
drinking water 飲み水 nomimizu
drive 運転する unten suru
driver 運転手 untenshu
driving licence 運転免許 unten menkyo
drop 落とす otosu
drug (medicine) 薬 kusuri
drug (narcotic) 麻薬 mayaku

drunk 酔った yotta
dry 乾いた kawaita
dry cleaner's ドライクリーナー dorai kurina
dryer ドライアー doraia
duck アヒル ahiru
due 締め切り shimekiri
dull 鈍い nibui
dummy 偽物 nisemono
during 〜の間に ...no aida ni
dust 埃 hokori
dustbin ゴミ箱 gomibako
duster ふきん fukin
dustpan ちりとり chiritori
Dutch, Dutchman, Dutchwoman オランダ人、オランダ人男性、オランダ人女性 orandajin, orandajin dansei, orandajin jyosei
duty-free 埃のない hokori no nai
duvet 布団 futon
duvet cover 布団カバー futon kaba
dye (n) 染料 senryo
dye (vb) 染める someru
dynamo 発電機 hatsudenki

E
each それぞれ sorezore
eagle 鷲 washi
ear 耳 mimi
earache 耳痛 jitsu
earphones イヤフォン ia fon
earrings イアリング ia ringu
earth 地球 chikyu
earthquake 地震 jishin
east 東 higashi

Easter 復活際 fukkatsusai
Easter egg イースターエッグ isuta eggu
easy 簡単な kantanna
eat 食べる taberu
EC 欧州共同体 oshu kyodotai
economy 経済 keizai
economy class エコノミークラス ekonomi kurasu
edge 端 hashi
eel うなぎ unagi
egg 卵 tamago
either ... or 〜か〜 ...ka...ka
elastic ゴムひも gomuhimo
elbow 肘 hiji
electric 電気の denkino
electrician 電気技師 denkigishi
electricity 電気 denki
elevator エレベーター erebeta
embassy 大使館 taishikan
emergency 緊急の kinkyuno
emergency exit 非常口 hijoguchi
empty 空の karano
end 終わり owari
engaged (occupied) 使用中 shiyochu
engaged (to be married) 婚約している konyakushiteiru
engine エンジン enjin
engineer 技師 gishi
England イギリス igirisu

English (language) 英語 eigo
English Channel イギリス海峡 igirisu kaikyo
English, Englishman/woman イギリス人、イギリス人男性、イギリス人女性 igirisujin igirisujin dansei, igirisujin jyosei
enjoy 楽しむ tanoshimu
enlargement 拡大 kakudai
enough 十分な jyubun na
enquiry 質問 shitsumon
enquiry desk 受付所 uketsukejyo
enter 入る hairu
entrance 入り口 iriguchi
entrance fee 入場料 nyujyoryo
envelope 封筒 futo
epilepsy てんかん tenkan
epileptic てんかん患者 tenkan kanja
equipment 道具 dogu
error エラー era
escalator エスカレーター esukareta
escape 逃げる nigeru
especially 特に tokuni
essential 重要である jyuyo dearu
estate agent 不動産屋 fudosanya
Estonia エストニア esutonia
EU 欧州連合 oshu rengo
Europe ヨーロッパ yoroppa
European ヨーロッパ人 yoroppa jin

even (equal) 等しい hitoshii
even (flat) 平らな tairana
evening 夕方 yugata
eventually やがて yagate
every いつも itsumo
everyone 皆 mina
everything 全て subete
everywhere どこでも dokodemo
exactly 正確に seikakuni
examination 試験 shiken
example, for example 例 rei
excellent すばらしい subarashii
except 〜を除いて ...o nozoite
excess luggage 超過荷物 choka nimotsu
exchange 交換する kokan suru
exciting 楽しい tanoshii
exclude 除く nozoku
excursion 周遊 shuyu
excuse 言い訳 iiwake
Excuse me! すみません sumimasen
exhaust pipe マフラー mafura
exhausted 疲れた tsukareta
exhibition 展示会 tenjikai
exit 出口 deguchi
expect 期待する kitai suru
expenses 消費 shohi
expensive 高価な kokana
experienced 経験のある keikennoaru

expire 期限切れ kigengire
explain 説明する setsumei suru
explosion 爆発 bakuhatsu
export 輸出する yushutsu suru
exposure 露出 roshutsu
express (train) 急行 kyuko
extension 延長 encho
extension lead 延長コード encho kodo
extra 余分の yobun no
extraordinary 並外れた namihazureta
eye 目 me
eye drops 目薬 megusuri
eye make-up remover 化粧落とし kesho otoshi
eye shadow アイシャドウ aishado

F
fabric 繊維 seni
façade 外観 gaikan
face 顔 kao
factory 工場 kojyo
faint 気絶 kizetsu
fair (fête) 祭り matsuri
fair (hair colour) 淡い色 awaiiro
fairly かなり kanari
fake (n) 偽物 nisemono
fake (vb) 振りをする furi o suru
fall 落ちる ochiru
family 家族 kazoku
famous 有名 yumei

fan 扇風機 senpuki
fanbelt ファンベルト fan beruto
far (adv) 遠くに toku ni
fare 運賃 unchin
farm 農地 nochi
farmer 農家 noka
farmhouse 農場 nojyo
fashionable 流行の hayarino
fast 早い hayai
fasten 締める shimeru
fasten seatbelt シートベルトを締める shitoberuto o shimeru
fat 太っている futotte iru
father 父 chichi
father-in-law 義理の父 giri no chichi
fatty 脂っこい aburakoi
fault 誤り ayamari
faulty 欠陥がある kekkanga aru
favourite お気に入りの okini irino
fax ファックス fakusu
February 2月 nigatsu
feed 食料を与える shokuryo wo ataeru
feel 感じる kanjiru
feet 足 ashi
female 性 jyosei
fence フェンス fensu
fender フェンダー fenda
ferry フェリー feri
festival 祭り matsuri
fetch 取ってくる tottekuru
fever 熱 netsu

few, a few 少し sukoshi
fiancé, fiancée 婚約者 konyakusha
field 広場 hiroba
fight (n) 戦い tatakai
fight (vb) 戦う tatakau
file (folder) ファイル fairu
file (tool) やすり yasuri
fill, fill in, fill up 満たす mitasu
fillet ヒレ hire
filling (sandwich) 中身 nakami
filling (tooth) 詰め物 tsumemono
film (camera) フイルム fuirumu
film (movie) 映画 eiga
film processing 現像処理 genzo shori
filter フィルター firuta
filthy 汚い kitanai
find 見つける mitsukeru
fine (n) 良い yoi
finger 指 yubi
finish 終わる owaru
fire 火 hi
fire brigade 消防隊 shoubotai
fire exit 非常口 hijyoguchi
fire extinguisher 消火器 shokaki
first, at first 最初に saishoni
first aid 応急手当 okyu teate
first-aid kit 救急箱 kyukyubako

first class ファーストクラス fasuto kurasu
first floor 1階 ikkai
first name 名前 namae
fish 魚 sakana
fishing permit 釣りの許可 tsurino kyoka
fishing rod 釣り竿 tsurizao
fishmonger's 漁師 ryoshi
fit (healthy) 健康 kenko
fitting room 着替え室 kigaeshitsu
fix 修理する shuri suru
fizzy 泡立つ awadatsu
flannel フランネル furanneru
flash (of lightning) 稲光 inabikari
flashlight 懐中電灯 kaichudento
flask フラスコ瓶 furasuko bin
flat 平ら taira
flat battery バッテリー切れ batteri gire
flat tyre パンク panku
flavour 味 aji
flaw 欠陥 kekkan
flea ノミ nomi
flight フライト furaito
flip flops サンダル sandaru
flippers 足ヒレ ashihire
flood 洪水 kozui
floor (of room) 床 yuka
floor (storey) 階 kai
floorcloth 床雑巾 yukazokin
florist 花屋 hanaya
flour 小麦粉 komugiko
flower 花 hana
flu 風邪 kaze

fluent 流暢 ryucho
fly 飛ぶ tobu
fog 霧 kiri
folk 民芸 mingei
follow 〜について行く ...ni tsuiteiku
food 食べ物 tabemono
food poisoning 食中毒 shokuchudoku
food shop 食品店 shokuhinten
foot 足 ashi
football (soccer) サッカー sakka
football match サッカーの試合 sakka no shiai
footpath 小道 komichi
for 〜のために ...no tameni
forbidden 禁じられている kinjirarete iru
forehead 額 hitai
foreign 外国の gaikoku no
foreigner 外国人 gaikokujin
forest 森 mori
forget 忘れる wasureru
fork フォーク foku
form (document) 用紙 yoshi
form (shape) 形 katachi
formal フォーマル fomaru
fortnight 2週間 ni shukan
fortress 砦 toride
fortunately 幸運にも koun nimo
fountain 噴水 funsui
four-wheel drive 四駆 yonku

fox 狐 kitsune
fracture ひび hibi
frame フレーム furemu
France フランス furansu
free 自由な jiyuna
freelance 自由契約の jiyukeiyakuno
freeway 高速道路 kosoku doro
freezer 冷凍庫 reitoko
French, Frenchman/woman フランス人、フランス人男性、フランス人女性 furansujin, furansujin dan sei, furansujin jyosei
French fries フレンチフライ furenchi furai
frequent 頻繁に hinpan ni
fresh 新鮮 shinsen
Friday 金曜日 kinyobi
fridge 冷蔵庫 reizoko
fried 揚げた ageta
friend 友達 tomodachi
friendly 親切な shinsetsu na
frog カエル kaeru
from (origin) 〜から ...kara
from (time) 〜から ...kara
front 前 mae
frost 霜 shimo
frozen 凍った kotta
fruit 果物 kudamono
fruit juice フルーツジュース furutsu jyusu
fry 揚げる ageru
frying pan フライパン furaipan
fuel 燃料 nenryo
fuel gauge 燃料計 nenryokei

full いっぱいの ippai no
full board 3食付き sanshokutsuki
fun (adj) 楽しい tanoshii
fun (n) 愉快 yukai
funeral 葬式 soshiki
funicular ケーブルカー keburuka
funny おもしろい omoshiroi
fur 毛皮 kegawa
fur coat 毛皮のコート kegawa no koto
furnished 家具付き kagutsuki
furniture 家具 kagu
further より遠くへ yori toku e
fuse ヒューズ hyuzu
fuse box ヒューズボックス hyuzu bokkusu
future 将来 shorai

G

Gallery ギャラリー gyarari
gallon ガロン garon
game ゲーム gemu
garage ガレージ gareji
garden 庭 niwa
garlic にんにく ninniku
gas ガス gasu
gas cooker ガスクッカー gasu kukaa
gate ゲート geto
gay ホモ homo
gay bar ゲイバー gei ba
gear ギア gia
gear lever ギアレバー gia reba
gearbox ギアボックス gia bokusu

general 概要 gaiyo
generous 寛大 kandai
Geneva ジュネーブ jyunebu
gents' toilet 男子トイレ danshi toire
genuine 本物の honmonono
German ドイツ人 doitsujin
German measles 風疹 fushin
Germany ドイツ doitsu
get 得る eru
get off 下りる oriru
get on 乗る noru
get up 上がる agaru
gift ギフト gifuto
girl 女の子 onna no ko
girlfriend ガールフレンド garu furendo
give あげる ageru
give back 返す kaesu
glacier 氷河 hyoga
glad うれしい ureshi
glass (tumbler) コップ koppu
glasses (spectacles) 眼鏡 megane
gloomy 陰気な inki na
gloves 手袋 tebukuro
glue 糊 nori
go 行く iku
go (by car) 車で行く kuruma de iku
go (on foot) 歩いて行く aruite iku
go away 去る saru
go back 戻る modoru
goat ヤギ yagi
God 神様 kamisama

goggles ゴーグル goguru
gold 金 kin
golf club (place) ゴルフ場 gorufu jyo
golf club (stick) ゴルフクラブ gorufu kurabu
golf course ゴルフコース gorufu kosu
good よい yoi
good afternoon こんにちは kon nichiwa
good day こんにちは kon nichiwa
good evening こんばんは kon banwa
Good Friday 聖金曜日 sei kin yobi
good luck 頑張って ganbatte
good morning おはよう ohayo
good night おやす oyasumi
goodbye さようなら sayonara
goose ガチョウ gacho
Gothic ゴシック goshikku
government 政府 seifu
gradually 徐々に jyojyoni
gram グラム guramu
grammar 文法 bumpo
grand 壮大な sodaina
granddaughter 孫娘 magomusume
grandfather おじいさん ojii san
grandmother おばあさん obaa san
grandparents 祖父母 sofubo
grandson 孫息子 magomusuko
grapes 葡萄 budo
grass 草 kusa
grated おろした oroshita
grateful 感謝する kansha suru
gravy 肉汁 nikujiru
greasy 油っぽい aburappoi
great すばらしい subarashii
Great Britain 英国 eikoku
Greece ギリシャ girisha
Greek ギリシャ人 girisha jin
green 緑 midori
greengrocer's 八百屋 yaoya
greeting 挨拶 aisatsu
grey 灰色 hai iro
grilled 網焼きの amiyaki no
ground 地面 jimen
ground floor 1階 ikkai
group グループ gurupu
guarantee 保証 hosho
guard 保護 hogo
guest お客様 okyaku sama
guesthouse ゲストハウス gesuto hausu
guide ガイド gaido
guide book ガイドブック gaido boku
guided tour ガイド付きツアー gaido tsuki tsua
guitar ギター gitaa
gun 銃 jyu
gym ジム gimu

H

hail 歓迎 kangei
hair 髪 kami
hairbrush ヘアブラシ hea burashi
haircut 整髪 seihatsu
hairdresser 美容師 biyoshi
hairdresser's 美容師の biyoshi no
hairdryer ヘアドライヤー hea doraia
half (n) 半分 hanbun
hall 玄関 genkan
ham ハム hamu
hamburger ハンバーガー hambaga
hammer ハンマー hanma
hand 手 te
hand luggage 手荷物 tenimotsu
handbag ハンドバッグ hando baggu
handbrake ハンドブレーキ hando bureki
handicapped 体の不自由な karada no fujiyu na
handkerchief ハンカチ hankachi
handle ハンドル handoru
handmade 手作り tezukuri
handsome ハンサム hansamu
hang up (phone) 電話を切る denwa o kiru
hanger ハンガー hanga
hang-gliding ハングライディング hangu raidingu
hangover 二日酔い futsuka yoi
happen 〜が起こる ...ga okoru
happy 幸せ shiawase
Happy Easter! ハッピーイースター! happi isuta!
Happy New Year! あけましておめでとう。! amemashite omedeto!
harbour 港 minato
hard きつい kitsui
hard disk ハードディスク hado disuku
hardly ほとんど〜ない hatondo...nai
hardware shop 金物屋 kanamono ya
harvest 収穫 shukaku
hat 帽子 boshi
have 持っている motteiru
have to 〜しなければならない。 ...shinakereba naranai
hay fever 花粉症 kafunsho
hazelnut ヘーゼルナッツ hezerunattsu
he 彼 kare
head 頭 atama
headache 頭痛 zutsu
headlight/s ヘッドライト heddo raito
headphones ヘッドフォン heddo fon

health food shop 健康食品店 kenko shokuhin ten
healthy 健康な kenko na
hear 聞く kiku
hearing aid 補聴器 hochoki
heart 心臓 shinzo
heart attack 心臓発作 shinzo hossa
heartburn 胸焼 muneyake
heat 熱 netsu
heater ヒーター hiita
heating 暖房 dambo
heavy 重い omoi
heel かかと kakato
height 高さ takasa
helicopter ヘリコプター herikoputa
helmet ヘルメット herumetto
Help! 助けて! tasukete!
help 助ける tasukeru
hem すそ suso
her 彼女 kanojyo
herbal tea ハーブティー habu ti
herbs ハーブ habu
here ここで kokode
hernia ヘルニア herunia
hide 隠れる kakureru
high 高い takai
high blood pressure 高血圧 koketsuatsu
high chair 高椅子 takaisu
him, to him 彼、彼に kare, kare ni
hip お尻 oshiri

hip replacement 人工股関節置換手術 jinko kokansetsu chikan shujyutsu
hire 借りる kariru
hire car レンタカー rentaka
his 彼の kare no
historic 歴史上の rekishijyo no
history 歴史 rekishi
hit 打つ utsu
hitchhike ヒッチハイク hicchi haiku
hold 握る nigiru
hole 穴 ana
holidays 休み yasumi
holy 神聖な shinsei na
home 家 ie
homesickness ホームシック homu shikku
homosexual ホモセクシャル homo sekusharu
honest 正直 shojiki
honey 蜂蜜 hachimitsu
honeymoon 新婚旅行 shinkon ryoko
hood (car) ボンネット bonnetto
hood (garment) 頭巾 zukin
hope 願い negai
hopefully 願わくば negawakuba
horn (animal) 角 tsuno
horn (car) クラクション kurakushon
horse 馬 uma
horse racing 競馬 keiba
horse riding 乗馬 jyoba

ENGLISH → JAPANESE

hose pipe ホース hosu
hospital 病院 byoin
hospitality 親切なもてなし shinsetsu na motenashi
hostel ホステル hosuteru
hot 暑い atsui
hot spring 温泉 onsen
hot-water bottle 湯たんぽ yutampo
hour 時間 jikan
hourly 1時間おきに ichi jikan okini
hourly 毎時間の mai jikan no
house 家 ie
house wine ハウスワイン hausu wain
housework 家事 kaji
hovercraft ホバークラフト hoba kurafuto
How? どのようにして? donoyonishite?
How are you? 元気ですか? genki desuka?
How do you do? はじめまして hajimemashite?
How many? いくつ必要ですか? ikutsu hitsuyo desuka?
How much is it? いくらですか? ikura desuka?
humid 蒸し暑い mushi atsui
humour ユーモア yumoa
Hungarian ハンガリー人 hangari jin
Hungary ハンガリー hangari
hungry 空腹の kufukuno
hunt 狩る karu
hunting permit 狩猟免許 shuryo menkyo
hurry 急ぐ isogu
hurt 痛む itamu
hurts 怪我 kega
husband 夫 otto
hydrofoil 水中翼 suichu yoku
hypodermic needle 皮下注射器 hika chushaki

I
ice 氷 kori
ice cream アイスクリーム aisu kurimu
ice rink スケートリンク suketo rinku
ice skates アイススケート aisu suketo
iced coffee アイスコーヒー aisu kohi
idea アイデア aidea
identity card 身分証明書 mibun shomeisho
if もし moshi
if not もしだめなら moshi damenara
ignition 発火 hakka
ignition key エンジンキー enjin ki
ill 病気で byoki de
illness 病気 byoki
immediately すぐに suguni
important 重要な jyuyo na
impossible 不可能 fukano
improve 改善する kaizen suru
in ～の中に ...no nakani
inch インチ inchi

included 〜を含む ...o fukumu
inconvenience 不便 fuben
incredible すごい sugoi
Indian インド人 indo jin
indicator 指示器 shijiki
indigestion 消化不良 shoka furyo
indoor pool 屋内プール okunai puru
indoors 屋内 okunai
infection 感染 kansen
infectious 伝染性の densensei no
inflammation 炎症 ensho
inflate 膨らむ fukuramu
informal 形式張らない keishiki baranai
information 情報 jyoho
ingredients 材料 zairyo
injection 注射 chusha
injured 怪我する kega suru
injury 怪我 kega
ink インク inku
in-laws 姻戚 inseki
inn 宿屋 shukuya
inner tube インナーチューブ inna chubu
insect 虫 mushi
insect bite 虫さされ mushi sasare
insect repellent 虫除け mushi yoke
inside 内側 uchigawa
insist 主張する shucho suru
insomnia 不眠症 fuminsho
inspect 〜を検査する ...o kensa suru

instant coffee インスタントコーヒー insutanto kohi
instead 〜の代わりに ...no kawarini
insulin インシュリン inshurin
insurance 保険 hoken
intelligent 知性のある chisei no aru
intend 〜するつもりである ...suru tsumori de aru
interesting 面白い omoshiroi
international 国際的な kokusaiteki na
interpreter 通訳者 tsuyakusha
intersection 交差点 kosaten
interval 間隔 kankaku
into 〜の中に ...no nakani
introduce 紹介する shokai suru
investigation 調査 chosa
invitation 招待 shotai
invite 招待する shotai suru
invoice 請求書 seikyusho
Ireland アイルランド airurando
Irish, Irishman/woman アイルランド人、アイルランド人男性、アイルランド人女性 airurandojin, airudandojin dansei, airurandojin josei
iron (appliance) アイロン airon
iron (metal) 鉄 tetsu
iron 強固さ kyoko sa
ironing board アイロン台 airon dai

ironmonger's 金物屋 kanamono ya
is 〜です。...desu
island 島 shima
it (dir object) それ sore
it (indir object) あれ are
it (subject) これ kore
Italian イタリア人 itariajin
Italian (language) イタリア語 itariago
Italy イタリア itaria
itch (n) かゆい kayui
itch (v) 〜したい ...shitai

J

jack (car) ジャッキ jakki
jacket ジャケット jaketo
jam ジャム jamu
jammed 混雑した konzatsu shita
January 1月 ichi gatsu
jar ジャー jya
jaundice 黄疸 otan
jaw 顎 ago
jealous 嫉妬して shitto shite
jelly ゼリー zeri
jellyfish くらげ kurage
jersey ジャージ jyaji
Jew, Jewish ユダヤ教徒、ユダヤ人 yudayakyoto, yudayajin
jeweller's 宝石店 hosekiten
jewellery 宝石 hoseki
job 仕事 shigoto
jog (n) ジョギング jogingu
jog (vb) ジョギングする jogingu suru

join 参加する sanka suru
joint 接合 setsugo
joke ジョーク jyoku
journey 旅 tabi
joy 楽しみ tanoshimi
judge 裁判官 saibankan
jug 水入れ mizuire
juice ジュース jyusu
July 7月 shichi gatsu
jump (n) ジャンプ jampu
jump (vb) ジャンプする jampu suru
jump leads ジャンパー線 jampa sen
jumper ジャンパー jampa
junction ジャンクション jankushon
June 6月 roku gatsu
just (fair) 公平 kohei
just (only) ちょうど chodo

K

keep 維持する iji suru
Keep the change! お釣りはいりません! otsuri wa irimasen!
kettle やかん yakan
key 鍵 kagi
key ring キーホルダー ki horuda
kick 蹴る keru
kidney 腎臓 jinzo
kill 殺す korosu
kilo キロ kiro
kilogram キログラム kiroguramu
kilometre キロメーター kirometa

kind 親切な shinsetsu na
king 王 oh
kiosk キオスク kiosuku
kiss (n) キス kisu
kiss (vb) キスする kisu suru
kitchen 台所 daidokoro
kitchenette 簡易台所 kan i daidokoro
knee 膝 hiza
knickers ニッカボッカー nikka boka
knife ナイフ naifu
knit 編む amu
knitting needle 編み棒 amibo
knitwear ニットウェア nitto uea
knock ノックする nokku suru
knock down 倒す taosu
knock over 引っくり返す hikkuri kaesu
know 知っている shitte iru

L
label ラベル raberu
lace レース resu
ladder はしご hashigo
ladies' toilet 女性用トイレ jyoseiyo toire
ladies' wear 婦人服 fujin fuku
lady 女性 jyosei
lager ラガー raga
lake 湖 mizu umi
lamb 羊 hitsuji
lamp ランプ rampu
land 土地 tochi
landlady 地主 jinushi
landlord 地主 jinushi

landslide 地すべり jisuberi
lane 車線 shasen
language 言語 gengo
language course 語学コース gogaku kosu
large 大きい ohkii
last 最後 saigo
last night 夕べ yube
late 遅く osoku
later 後で atode
Latvia ラトビア ratobia
laugh (vb) 笑う warau
laugh (n) 笑い声 waraigoe
launderette, laundromat コインランドリー koin randori
laundry 洗濯 sentaku
lavatory 洗面所 senmenjyo
law 法律 horitsu
lawyer 弁護士 bengoshi
laxative 下剤 gezai
lazy 怠けている namakete iru
lead (metal) 鉛 namari
lead-free 無鉛 muen
leaf 葉 ha
leaflet チラシ chirashi
leak (n) 漏電 roden
leak (v) 漏れる moreru
learn 学ぶ manabu
lease (n) 賃貸 chintai
lease (vb) 賃貸する chintai suru
leather 皮 kawa
leave 発つ tatsu
leek ねぎ negi
left, to the left 左、左に hidari, hidari ni

left-hand drive 左ハンドル
 hidari handoru
left-handed 左利き
 hidari kiki
leg 脚 ashi
lemon レモン remon
lemonade レモネード
 remonedo
lend 貸す kasu
lens レンズ renzu
lentil レンティル rentiru
lesbian レズビアン rezubian
less 少なめ sukuname
lesson 稽古 keiko
let (allow) 許可する
 kyoka suru
let (hire) 貸し出し kashidashi
letter 手紙 tegami
letterbox 郵便受け
 yubin uke
lettuce レタス retasu
level crossing 踏切
 fumikiri
lever レバー reba
library 図書館 toshokan
licence 免許 menkyo
lid 蓋 futa
lie (n) 嘘 uso
lie (vb) 嘘をつく
 uso wo tsuku
lie down 横になる
 yoko ni naru
life 人生 jinsei
life belt 安全ベルト
 anzen beruto
life insurance 生命保険
 seimei hoken
life jacket 救命胴衣
 kyumei doi

lifeguard ライフガード
 raifu gado
lift (elevator) エレベーター
 erebeta
lift 〜を持ち上げる
 wo mochiageru
light (colour) 明るい akarui
light (weight) 軽い karui
light (n) 光 hikari
light (v) 光る hikaru
light bulb 電球 denkyu
lightning 雷 kaminari
like (enjoy) 好き suki
like (as) 〜のような
 ...no yona
lime ライム raimu
line 線 sen
linen リンネル rinneru
lingerie 下着 shitagi
lion ライオン raion
lipstick 口紅 kuchibeni
liqueur リキュール rikyuru
list 表 hyo
listen 聴く kiku
Lithuania リトアニア ritoania
litre リットル rittoru
litter (n) ゴミ gomi
litter (vb) ゴミの投げ捨て
 gomi no nagesute
little 少し sukoshi
live 住む sumu
lively 元気な genki na
liver 肝臓 kanzo
living room リビングルーム
 ribingurumu
loaf ひと塊 hito katamari
lobby ロビー robi
lobster 伊勢海老 iseebi
local 地元 jimoto

lock (n) 鍵 kagi
lock (vb) 鍵を閉める kagi wo shimeru
lock in 閉じ込める tojikomeru
lock out 締め出す shimedasu
locked in 閉じ込められる tojikome rareru
locker ロッカー rokka
lollipop 棒つきキャンディー botsuki kyandi
long (adj) 長い nagai
long (desire) 願う negau
long-distance call 長距離電話 chokyori denwa
look after 世話する sewa suru
look at 〜を見る ...o miru
look for 探す sagasu
look forward to 待ちわびる machiwabiru
loose ゆるい yurui
lorry トラック torakku
lose 負ける makeru
lost 迷った mayotta
lost property 忘れ物 wasuremono
lot くじ kuji
loud うるさい urusai
lounge ラウンジ raunji
love (n) 愛 ai
love (v) 愛する aisuru
lovely すごくいい sugoku ii
low 低い hikui
low fat 低脂肪 teishibo
luck 運 un
luggage 荷物 nimotsu

luggage rack 手荷物棚 tenimotsu dana
luggage tag 手荷物札 tenimotsu fuda
luggage trolley トローリー torori
lump こぶ kobu
lunch 昼食 chushoku
lung 肺 hai
Luxembourg ルクセンブルグ rukusenburugu
luxury 贅沢品 zeitakuhin

M
machine 機械 kikai
mad 狂った kurutta
made 作られた tsukurareta
magazine 雑誌 zasshi
maggot 蛆虫 ujimushi
magnet 磁石 jishaku
magnifying glass 虫眼鏡 mushimegane
maid メイド meido
maiden name 旧姓 kyusei
mail (n) 郵便 yubin
mail (vb) 郵送する yuso suru
main 主要な shuyo na
main course メインコース mein kosu
main post office 中央郵便局 chuo yubinkyoku
main road 大通り oh dori
mains switch メインスイッチ mein suicchi
make 作る tsukuru
male 男性 dansei
man 人 hito
man-made fibre 化学繊維 kagakuseni

manager マネージャー manejya
manual マニュアル manyuaru
many たくさん takusan
map 地図 chizu
marble 大理石 dairiseki
March 3月 san gatsu
market 市場 ichiba
marmalade マーマレード mamaredo
married 結婚している kekkon shiteiru
marsh 沼地 numachi
mascara マスカラ masukara
mashed potatoes マッシュポテト mashu poteto
mask マスク masuku
Mass (rel) ミサ misa
mast マスト masuto
match (sport) 試合 shiai
matches (for lighting) マッチ macchi
material 物質 busshitsu
matter 事態 jitai
matter – it doesn't matter 気にしないで下さい kinishinaide kudasai
mattress マットレス mattoresu
May 5月 go gatsu
may 〜かもしれない ...kamo shirenai
maybe たぶん tabun
mayonnaise マヨネーズ mayonezu
me 私 watashi

meal ご飯 gohan
mean (intend) 〜を意味する ...wo imi suru
mean (nasty) 意地悪な ijiwaruna
measles はしか hashika
measure (n) 大きさ okisa
measure (vb) 測る hakaru
meat 肉 niku
mechanic メカニック mekanikku
medical insurance 医療保険 iryo hoken
medicine (drug) 薬 kusuri
medicine (science) 薬学 yakugaku
medieval 中世の chusei no
Mediterranean 地中海 chichukai
medium 中間 chukan
medium dry wine 中辛ワイン chukara wain
medium rare (meat) ミディアムレア midiamu rea
medium sized M寸 emu sun
meet 会う au
meeting ミーティング mitingu
melon メロン meron
melt 溶ける tokeru
men 人 hito
mend 修繕 shuzen
meningitis 髄膜炎 zuimakuen
menswear 紳士服 shinshi fuku
mention 述べる noberu
menu メニュー menyu

meringue メレンゲ merenge
message メッセージ messeji
metal 金属 kinzoku
meter 計測器 keisokuki
metre メートル metoru
metro 地下鉄 chikatetsu
microwave oven 電子レンジ denshi renji
midday 日中 nicchu
middle 中心 chushin
midnight 深夜 shinya
might 〜かもしれない ...kamo shirenai
migraine 偏頭痛 henzutsu
mile マイル mairu
milk 牛乳 gyunyu
minced meat ひき肉 hikiniku
mind 精神 seishin
mineral water ミネラルウォーター mineraru uota
minister 大臣 daijin
mint ミント minto
minute 分 fun
mirror 鏡 kagami
Miss 〜さん ...san
missing 見つからない mitsukaranai
mist 霧 kiri
mistake 失敗 shippai
misunderstanding 誤解 gokai
mix ミックス mikkusu
mix-up 混同 kondo
mix up 混同する kondo suru
mobile phone 携帯電話 keitai denwa

moisturizer 保湿剤 hoshitsuzai
moment 瞬間 shunkan
monastery 修道院 shudoin
Monday 月曜日 getsuyo
money お金 okane
money belt マネーベルト mane beruto
money order 送金為替 sokin kawase
month 月 tsuki
monthly 毎月 maitsuki
monument 記念碑 kinenhi
moon 月 tsuki
mooring 停泊 teihaku
more もっと motto
morning 朝 asa
mosque モスク mosuku
mosquito 蚊 ka
most ほとんどの hotondono
mostly ほとんど hotondo
moth 蛾 ga
mother 母 haha
mother-in-law 義理の母 giri no haha
motor モーター mota
motorbike バイク baiku
motorboat モーターボート mota boto
motorway 高速道路 kosoku doro
mountain 山 yama
mountain rescue 山岳救助 sangaku kyujyo
mountaineering 登山 tozan
mouse ねずみ nezumi
moustache ひげ hige
mouth 口 kuchi

mouth ulcer 口内 konaien
mouthwash うがい ugai
move 動く ugoku
move house 引っ越す hikkosu
Mr ～さん ...san
Mrs/Ms ～さん ...san
much たくさん takusan
mud 泥 doro
mug マグ magu
mugged 強盗にあう goto ni au
mumps おたふく風邪 otafuku kaze
muscle 筋肉 kinniku
museum 博物館 hakubutsukan
mushroom マッシュルーム masshurumu
musician 音楽家 ongakuka
Muslim イスラム教徒 isuramu kyoto
mussel ムール貝 muru gai
must ～しなくてはならない。 ...shinakutewa naranai
mustard マスタード masutado
mutton マトン maton
my 私の watashi no
myself 私 watashi

N
nail 爪 tsume
nail brush 爪ブラシ tsume burashi
nail file 爪やすり tsume yasuri
nail polish/varnish マニキュア液 manikyua eki
nail polish remover マニキュア落とし manikyua otoshi
nail scissors 爪きり tsumekiri
name 名前 namae
nanny 子守 komori
napkin ナプキン napukin
nappy おしめ oshime
narrow 狭い semai
nasty 意地悪な ijiwaruna
national 国民 kokumin
nationality 国籍 kokuseki
natural 自然の shizen no
nature 自然 shizen
nature reserve 自然公園 shizenkoen
nausea 吐き気 hakike
navy 海軍 kaigun
navy blue ネイビーブルー neibi buru
near (adj) 近い chikai
near (vb) 近づく chikazuku
nearby (adj) 近くの chikaku no
nearby (adv) 近くに chikaku ni
nearly もう少しで mo sukoshide
necessary 必要 hitsuyo
neck 首 kubi
necklace ネックレス nekkuresu
need (vb) 必要です hitsuyo desu
need (n) 必要性 hitsuyosei
needle 針 hari
neighbour 近所 kinjyo

neither ... nor
～のどちらでもない
...no dochirademo nai
nephew 甥 oi
nest 巣 su
net 網 ami
Netherlands オランダ
oranda
never 絶対しない
zettai shinai
new 新しい atarashi
New Year 新年 shinnen
New Year's Eve 大晦日
omisoka
New Zealand, New Zealander ニュージーランド, ニュージーランド人
nyuji rando, nyuji rando jin
news ニュース nyusu
news stand 新聞売店
shimbun baiten
newspaper 新聞
shimbun
next 次の tsugino
nice よい yoi
niece 姪 mei
night, last night 夜、昨夜
yoru, sakuya
nightdress パジャマ
pajyama
no いいえ iie
nobody 誰も～ない
daremo...nai
noise 騒音 so on
noisy うるさい urusai
non-alcoholic
ノンアルコール non arukoru
non-smoking 禁煙 kin en
none ～でない ...de nai

north 北 kita
North Sea 北海 hokkai
Northern Ireland
北アイルランド
kita airurando
Norway ノルウェー noruwe
Norwegian ノルウェー人
noruwe jin
nose 鼻 hana
not ～でない ...de nai
note 気に留める kini tomeru
notebook ノート noto
notepaper メモ帳
memocho
nothing 皆無 kaimu
nothing else 他に何もない
hokani nanimo nai
noticeboard 掲示板
keijiban
novel 小説 shosetsu
November 11月
jyuichi gatsu
now 今 ima
nudist beach ヌードビーチ
nudo bichi
number 数 kazu
number plate
ナンバープレート
namba pureto
nurse 看護婦 kangofu
nursery (plants) 植木屋
uekiya
nursery school 保育園
hoikuen
nursery slope
初心者用のゲレンデ
shoshinshayo no gerende
nut ナッツ nattsu
nut (for bolt) ナット natto

O

oak オーク oku
oar オール oru
oats 麦 mugi
obtain 手に入れる teni ireru
occasionally たまに tamani
occupation 職業 shokugyo
occupied (e.g. toilet) 使用中 shiyochu
ocean 海 umi
October 10月 ju gatsu
odd (number) 奇数 kisu
odd (strange) 奇妙な kimyo na
of 〜の ...no
off から離れた ...kara hanareta
office 事務所 jimusho
often 頻繁に hinpan ni
oil オイル oiru
ointment 軟膏 nanko
OK オッケー okke
old 古い furui
old-age pensioner 老齢年金者 rorei nenkinsha
old-fashioned 古風な kofuna
olive オリーブ oribu
olive oil オリーブオイル oribu oiru
omelette オムレツ omuretsu
on 〜の上に ...no ueni
once 一度 ichido
one 1 ichi
one-way street 一方通行 ippo tsuko
onion たまねぎ tamanegi
only (however) ただし tadashi
only (adj) 唯一の yuiitsu no
open 開ける akeru
open ticket オープンチケット opun chiketto
opening times 開店時間 kaiten jikan
opera オペラ opera
operation 操作 sosa
operator (phone) 電話交換手 denwa kokanshu
ophthalmologist 眼科医 gankai
opposite 反対 hantai
optician 眼鏡屋 meganeya
or それとも soretomo
orange オレンジ orenji
orange juice オレンジジュース orenji jyusu
orchestra オーケストラ okesutora
order (n) 注文 chumon
order (vb) 注文する chumon suru
organic vegetables 有機栽培野菜 yukisaibai yasai
other 他の hokano
otherwise そうでなければ sode nakereba
our 私たちの watashitachi no
out 外 soto
out of order 故障中 kosho chu
outdoors アウトドア auto doa
outside 外側 sotogawa
outskirts 郊外 kogai

oven オーブン obun
ovenproof オーブン耐熱性の obun tainetsusei no
over 〜の向こうに ...no muko ni
over here ここで kokode
over there 向こうで muko de
overcharge 過剰請求 kajo seikyu
overcoat 上塗り uwanuri
overdone やり過ぎ yarisugi
overheat オーバーヒート oba hito
overnight 夜通しの yodoshi no
overtake 追い抜く oinuku
owe 借りがある kariga aru
owl ふくろう fukuro
owner 所有者 shoyusha

P

pacemaker ペースメーカー pesumeka
pacifier 調停者 choteisha
pack 包む tsutsumu
package 包み pakkeji
package holiday パッケージホリデー pakkeji horide
packet 小包 kozutsumi
padlock 南京錠 nankinjyo
page ページ peji
paid 支払済みの shiharaizumi no
pail バケツ baketsu

pain 痛み itami
painful 痛い itai
painkiller 痛み止め itamidome
paint (n) ペンキ penki
paint (vb) ペンキを塗る penki wo nuru
painting ペンキ塗り penki nuri
pair 対 tsui
palace 宮殿 kyuden
pale 青白い aojiroi
pan フライパン furaipan
pancake パンケーキ pankeki
panties パンティー panti
pants パンツ pantsu
pantyhose パンティーストッキング pantisutokkingu
paper 紙 kami
paper napkins 紙ナプキン kami napukin
parcel 小包 kozutsumi
Pardon? 何ですか? nandesuka
parents 両親 ryoshin
parents-in-law 義理の両親 giri no ryoshin
park (n) 公園 koen
park (vb) 駐車する chusha suru
parking disc パーキングディスク pakingu disuku
parking meter 駐車メーター chusha meta
parking ticket 駐車違反切符 chushaihan kippu

part 部分 bubun
partner (business)
　ビジネスパートナー
　bijinesu patona
partner (companion)
　パートナー patona
party (celebration)
　パーティー pati
party (political) 政党 seito
pass パス pasu
pass control パス制御
　pasu seigyo
passenger 乗客 jyokyaku
passport 旅券 ryoken
past 過去 kako
pastry ペストリー pesutori
path 小道 komichi
patient 患者 kanjya
pattern パターン patan
pavement 歩道 hodo
pay 払う harau
payment 支払い shihirai
payphone 公衆電話
　koshu denwa
pea 豆 mame
peach 桃 momo
peak 頂点 choten
peak rate 最高レート
　saiko reto
peanut ピーナッツ pinattsu
pear 梨 nashi
pearl 真珠 shinjyu
peculiar 変な hen na
pedal ペダル pedaru
pedestrian 歩行者
　hokosha
pedestrian crossing
　横断歩道 odanhodo
peel (vb) むく muku

peg くい kui
pen ペン pen
pencil 鉛筆 enpitsu
penfriend ペンフレンド
　pen furendo
peninsula 半島 hanto
people 人々 hitobito
pepper (vegetable)
　ピーマン piman
pepper (spice) コショウ
　kosho
per 〜につき ...nitsuki
perfect 完全 kanzen
performance
　パフォーマンス
　pafomansu
perfume 香水 kosui
perhaps 多分 tabun
period 期間 kikan
perm パーマをかける
　pama wo kakeru
permit (n) 許可 kyoka
permit (vb) 許可する
　kyoka suru
person 人 hito
pet ペット petto
petrol ガソリン gasorin
petrol can ガソリン缶
　gasorin kan
petrol station
　ガソリンスタンド
　gasorin sutando
pharmacist 薬剤師
　yakuzaishi
pharmacy 薬局 yakkyoku
phone 電話 denwa
phone booth
　公衆電話ボックス
　koshu denwa bokkusu

phone card テレフォンカード terefon kado
phone number 電話番号 denwa bango
photocopy コピー kopi
photograph (n) 写真 shashin
photograph (vb) 写真を撮る shashin wo toru
phrase book 会話集 kaiwashu
piano ピアノ piano
pickpocket すり suri
picnic ピクニック pikunikku
picture 写真 shashin
picture frame 額縁 gakubuchi
pie パイ pai
piece 一切れ hitokire
pig 豚 buta
pill 錠剤 jyozai
pillow 枕 makura
pillowcase 枕カバー makura kaba
pilot パイロット pairotto
pin ピン pin
pin number 暗証番号 ansho bango
pineapple パイナップル painappuru
pink ピンク pinku
pipe (plumbing) パイプ paipu
pipe (smoking) パイプ paipu
pity, It's a pity! 残念 zannen
place 場所 basho
plain 平原 heigen

plait 編んだもの anda mono
plane 飛行機 hikoki
plan 計画 keikaku
plaster 絆創膏 bansoko
plastic プラスチック purasuchikku
plastic bag ビニール袋 biniru bukuro
plate 皿 sara
platform プラットホーム purattofomu
play (n) 劇 geki
play (vb) 試合をする shiai wo suru
playground 広場 hiroba
please 喜ばせる yorokobaseru
pleased 喜ぶ yorokobu
Pleased to meet you! はじめまして! hajimemashite
plenty たくさん takusan
pliers ペンチ penchi
plug (bath) 栓 sen
plug (elec) コンセント konsento
plum プラム puramu
plumber 配管工 haikanko
p.m. (after noon) 午後 gogo
poached 落とし卵 otoshitamago
pocket ポケット poketto
points (car) 転轍機 tentetsuki
poison 毒 doku
poisonous 毒のある doku no aru

Poland ポーランド porando
Pole, Polish ポーランド人 porando jin
police 警察 keisatsu
police station 警察署 keisatsusho
policeman/woman 警察官 keisatsukan
polish (n) 光沢剤 kotakuzai
polish (vb) 磨く migaku
polite 礼儀正しい reigi tadashi
polluted 汚染された osensareta
pool プール puru
poor (impecunious) 貧しい mazushii
poor (quality) 質が悪い shitsu ga warui
poppy ケシ keshi
popular 人気のある ninnki no aru
population 人口 jinko
pork 豚肉 butaniku
port (harbour) 港 minato
port (wine) ポートワイン poto wain
porter ポーター pota
portion 部分 bubun
portrait ポートレート potoreto
Portugal ポルトガル porutogaru
Portuguese ポルトガル人 porutogaru jin
posh こぎれいな kogireina
possible 可能 kanou
post (n) ポスト posuto

post (vb) 郵便で送る yubin de okuru
post office 郵便局 yubinkyoku
post office box 私書箱 shishobako
postage 郵便料金 yubin ryokin
postage stamp 切手 kitte
postal code 郵便番号 yubin bango
postbox 郵便箱 yubin bako
postcard ポストカード posuto kado
poster ポスター posuta
postman/postwoman 郵便局員 yubinkyokuin
postpone 延期する enki suru
potato 芋 jyagaimo
pothole 道路の穴 doro no ana
pottery 陶器 toki
pound ポンド pondo
pour 注ぐ sosogu
powder 粉 kona
powdered milk 粉ミルク kona miruku
power cut 停電 teiden
practice 実践する jissen suru
practise 練習する renshu suru
pram ベビーカー bebiika
prawn 海老 ebi
pray 祈る inoru
prefer 〜を好む ...wo konomu

pregnant 妊娠している ninshin shiteiru
prescription 処方箋 shohosen
present (adj) 現在 genzai
present (n) プレゼント purezento
present (vb) 提示する teiji suru
pressure 圧力 atsuryoku
pretty 可愛い kawaii
price 値段 nedan
priest 牧師 bokushi
prime minister 首相 shusho
print 印刷する insatsu suru
printed matter 印刷物 insatsu butsu
prison 刑務所 keimusho
private プライベート puraibeto
prize 賞品 shohin
probably たぶん tabun
problem 問題 mondai
programme, program プログラム puroguramu
prohibited 禁止された kinshi sareta
promise (n) 約束 yakusoku
promise (vb) 約束する yakusoku suru
pronounce 発音する hatsuon suru
properly 正しく tadashiku
Protestant プロテスタント purotesutanto
public 公共の kokyono

public holiday 祝日 shukujitsu
pudding プリン purin
pull 引く hiku
pullover プルオーバ puruoba
pump ポンプ ponpu
puncture パンクする panku suru
puppet show 人形劇 ningyogeki
purple 紫 murasaki
purse 財布 saifu
push 押す osu
pushchair 乳母車 ubaguruma
put 置く oku
put up with ～に耐える ...ni taeru
pyjamas パジャマ pajama

Q

quality 質 shitsu
quantity 量 ryo
quarantine 検疫 ken eki
quarrel (n) 口論 koron
quarrel (vb) 口論する koron suru
quarter 4分の1 yon bun no 1
quay 埠頭 futo
queen 女王 jyoo
question 質問 shitsumon
queue (n) 列 retsu
queue (vb) 列に並ぶ retsu ni narabu
quickly 急いで isoide
quiet 静かに shizukani
quilt キルト kiruto
quite かなり kanari

R

rabbit ウサギ usagi
rabies 狂犬病 kyoken byo
race (people) 人種 jinshu
race (sport) レース resu
race course レースコース resu kosu
racket ラケット raketto
radiator ラジエーター rajieta
radio ラジオ rajio
radish 大根 daikon
rag 雑巾 zokin
railway 鉄道 tetsudo
railway station 駅 eki
rain 雨 ame
raincoat 雨合羽 ama gappa
raisin レーズン reizun
rake くま手 kumade
rape (n) 強姦 gokan
rape (vb) 強姦する gokan suru
rare めったにない mettani nai
rash 気の早い ki no hayai
raspberry ラズベリー razuberi
rat ねずみ nezumi
rate (of exchange) レート reto
raw 生 nama
razor かみそり kamisori
razor blade かみそりの刃 kamisori no ha
read 読む yomu
ready 用意ができて yoi ga dekite
real 本物 honmono
realize 気づく kizuku
really 本当に honto ni

rear-view mirror バックミラー bakkumira
reasonable 手ごろな tegorona
receipt 領収書 ryoshusho
receiver (tax) 受取人 uketorinin
receiver (telephone) 受話器 jyuwaki
recently 最近 saikin
reception 受付 uketsuke
receptionist 受付係り uketsuke gakari
recharge 再充電する saijyuden suru
recipe レシピ reshipi
recognize 〜だと分かる ...dato wakaru
recommend 推薦する suisen suru
record (legal) 記録 kiroku
record (music) レコード rekodo
red 赤 aka
red wine 赤ワイン aka wain
redcurrant レッドカラント reddokaranto
reduce 減らす herasu
reduction 縮小 shukusho
refund (n) 返金 henkin
refund (vb) 返金する henkin suru
refuse (n) ゴミ gomi
refuse (vb) 断る kotowaru
region 地区 chiku
register (n) 登録 toroku
register (vb) 登録する toroku suru

registered mail 書留 kakitome
registration form 登録用紙 toroku yoshi
registration number 登録番号 toroku bango
relative, relation 親戚 shinseki
remain 残る nokoru
remember 覚える oboeru
rent 賃貸する chintai suru
repair (vb) 修理する shuri suru
repair (n) 修理 shuri
repeat 繰り返す kurikaesu
reply (n) 返答 hento
reply (vb) 返答する hento suru
report (n) 報告 hokoku
report (vb) 報告する hokoku suru
request (n) 要請 yosei
request (vb) 要請する yosei suru
require 必要とする hitsuyo to suru
rescue (n) 救助 kyujyo
rescue (vb) 救助する kyujyo suru
reservation 予約 yoyaku
reserve 予約する yoyaku suru
resident 住人 junin
resort リゾート rizoto
rest (relax) 休憩する kyukei suru
rest (remainder) 残り nokori
retired 引退した intai shita

return 戻る modoru
return ticket 往復チケット ofuku chiketto
reverse (n) 逆 gyaku
reverse (vb) 逆さにする sakasani suru
reverse gear バックギア bakkugia
reverse-charge call コレクトコール korekuto koru
revolting 不快な fukaina
rheumatism リウマチ ryumachi
rib アバラ abara
ribbon リボン ribon
rice 米 kome
rich 裕福な yufukuna
ride 乗る noru
ridiculous 馬鹿げた bakageta
right 正しい tadashii
right-hand drive 右ハンドル migi handoru
ring 指輪 yubiwa
ring road 環状道路 kanjyo doro
rip-off ぼったくり bottakuri
ripe 熟した jyukushita
river 川 kawa
road 道路 doro
road accident 交通事故 kotsujiko
road map 道路地図 doro chizu
road sign 道路標識 doro hyoshiki
road works 道路工事 doro koji
roll 巻く maku

ENGLISH → JAPANESE

- **roof** 屋根 yane
- **roof-rack** ルーフラック rufurakku
- **room** 部屋 heya
- **rope** ロープ ropu
- **rose (flower)** バラ bara
- **rotten** 腐った kusatta
- **rough** 粗い arai
- **roughly** およそ oyoso
- **round** 丸い marui
- **roundabout** 回り道 mawarimichi
- **row (n)** 列 retsu
- **row (vb)** 漕ぐ kogu
- **royal** 王室の oshitsu no
- **rubber** ゴム gomu
- **rubbish** ゴミ gomi
- **rubella** 風疹 fushin
- **rudder** 舵 kaji
- **rug** 絨毯 jyutan
- **ruin** 破壊する hakai suru
- **ruler (for measuring)** 定規 jyogi
- **rum** ラム酒 ramu shu
- **run** 走る hashiru
- **rush** 急ぐ isogu
- **rusty** 錆びた sabita
- **rye bread** ライ麦パン raimugi pan

S

- **sad** 悲しい kanashii
- **saddle** サドル sadoru
- **safe (n)** 金庫 kinko
- **safe (adj)** 安全 anzen
- **safety belt** 安全ベルト anzen beruto
- **safety pin** 安全ピン anzen pin
- **sail** 航海 kokai
- **sailing** セイリング seiringu
- **salad** サラダ sarada
- **salad dressing** サラダドレッシング sarada doressingu
- **sale** 販売 hanbai
- **sales representative** 営業担当者 eigyo tantosha
- **salesperson** 販売員 hanbai in
- **salmon** 鮭 sake
- **salt** 塩 shio
- **same** 同じ onaji
- **sand** 砂 suna
- **sandals** サンダル sandaru
- **sandwich** サンドイッチ sandoicchi
- **sanitary pads** 生理用ナプキン seiriyo napukin
- **Saturday** 土曜日 doyo bi
- **sauce** ソース sosu
- **saucer** ソーサー sosa
- **sausage** ソーセージ soseji
- **save** 救う suku u
- **savoury** セイボリー seibori
- **say** 言う iu
- **scales** 秤 hakari
- **scarf** スカーフ sukafu
- **scenery** 景色 keshiki
- **school** 学校 gakko
- **scissors** ハサミ hasami
- **Scot, Scottish** スコットランド人 sukottorando jin
- **Scotland** スコットランド sukottorando

scrambled eggs スクランブルエッグ sukuranburu eggu
scratch (n) 引っかき傷 hikkaki kizu
scratch (vb) 引っかく hikkaku
screen スクリーン sukurin
screw ねじ neji
screwdriver ねじ回し nejimawashi
scrubbing brush たわし tawashi
scuba diving スキューバダイビング sukyuba daibingu
sea 海 umi
seagull かもめ kamome
seasick 船酔い funayoi
seaside 海岸 kaigan
season 季節 kisetsu
season ticket 定期券 teikiken
seasoning 調味料 chomiryo
seat 席 seki
seatbelt シートベルト shitoberuto
seaweed 海藻 kaiso
secluded 隔離された kakuri sareta
second 2番 niban
second-class 2等 nito
second-hand 中古 chuko
secretary 秘書 hisho
security guard 警備員 keibiin
see 見る miru
self-catering 自炊 jisui

self-employed 自営 jiei
self-service セルフサービス serufusabisu
sell 売る uru
sell-by date 賞味期限 shomikigen
send 送る okuru
senior citizen 高齢者 koreisha
sentence (grammar) 文章 bunsho
sentence (law) 判決 hanketsu
separate 別れる wakareru
September 9月 kugatsu
septic 腐敗物 fuhaibutsu
septic tank 浄化槽 jyokaso
serious 真剣 shinken
service サービス sabisu
service charge サービス料 sabisu ryo
serviette 紙ナプキン kami napukin
set menu セットメニュー setto menyu
several いくつかの ikutsukano
sew 縫う nuu
sex セックス sekkusu
shade 影 kage
shake 振る furu
shallow 浅い asai
shame 恥 haji
shampoo and set シャンプとセット shampu to setto
share 共有 kyoyu
sharp 鋭い surudoi
shave 剃る soru

she 彼女 kanojo
sheep 羊 hitsuji
sheet 用紙 yoshi
shelf 棚 tana
shellfish 甲殻類 kokakurui
sheltered 守られた mamorareta
shingle 小石 koishi
shingles シングルス shingurusu
ship 船 fune
shirt シャツ shatsu
shock absorber ショック　アブゾーバ shokku abuzoba
shoe 靴 kutsu
shoelace 靴紐 kutsuhimo
shop 店 mise
shop assistant 店員 ten in
shop window ショーウィンドー sho uwindo
shopping centre ショッピングセンター shoppingu senta
shore 海岸 kaigan
short 短い mijikai
short-cut 近道 chikamichi
short-sighted 近眼 kingan
shorts ショーツ shotsu
should 〜するべきです。 ...surubekidesu
shoulder 肩 kata
shout (n) 叫び sakebi
shout (vb) 叫ぶ sakebu
show (n) ショー sho
show (vb) 見せる miseru
shower シャワー shawa
shrimp 海老 ebi

shrink 縮む chijimu
shut 締める shimeru
shutter シャッター shatta
shy 恥かしがりや hazukashigariya
sick, I'm going to be sick! 気分が悪いです! kibun ga warui desu!
side 側面 sokumen
side dish サイドディッシュ saido disshu
sidewalk 歩道 hodo
sieve ふるい furui
sight 視界 shikai
sightseeing 観光 kanko
sign 標示 hyoji
signal シグナル sigunaru
signature 署名 shomei
signpost 標識 hyoshiki
silence 沈黙 chinmoku
silk 絹 kinu
silly 馬鹿げた bakageta
silver 銀 gin
similar 似た nita
simple 単純な tanjyunna
sing 歌う utau
singer 歌手 kashu
single シングル shinguru
single bed シングルベッド shinguru beddo
single room シングルルーム singuru rumu
single ticket 片道チケット katamichi chiketto
sink 流し nagashi
sister 姉妹 shimai
sister-in-law 義理の姉妹 giri no shimai

sit 座る suwaru
size サイズ saizu
skate (n) スケート suketo
skate (vb) スケートする suketo suru
skating rink スケートリンク suketo rinku
ski (n) スキー suki
ski (vb) スキーする suki suru
ski boot スキーブーツ suki butsu
ski jump スキージャンプ suki jampu
ski slope スキー場 suki jyo
skin 肌 hada
skirt スカート sukato
sky 空 sora
sledge そり sori
sleep 睡眠 suimin
sleeper, sleeping car 寝台車 shindaisha
sleeping bag 寝袋 nebukuro
sleeping pill 睡眠薬 suiminyaku
sleepy 眠い nemui
slice 一枚 ichimai
slide (n) 滑り台 suberidai
slide (vb) 滑る suberu
slip 滑る suberu
slippers スリッパ surippa
slippery 滑りやすい suberiyasui
Slovak スロバキア人 surobakia jin
Slovak Republic スロバキア共和国 surobakia kyowakoku
slow 遅い osoi
slowly ゆっくり yukkuri
small 小さい chisai
smell 匂い nioi
smile 微笑む hohoemu
smoke (n) 煙 kemuri
smoke (vb) 喫煙する kitsuen suru
smoked salmon スモークサーモン sumoku samon
snack スナック sunakku
snake 蛇 hebi
sneeze くしゃみ kushami
snore いびき ibiki
snorkel スノーケル sunokeru
snow, it is snowing 雪,雪が降っている yuki, yuki ga futteiru
soaking solution コンタクトレンズの保存液 kontakuto renzu no hozoneki
soap 石鹸 sekken
soap powder 粉石鹸 konasekken
sober しらふの shirafuno
socket (elec) ソケット soketto
socks 靴下 kutsushita
soda ソーダ soda
soft やわらかい yawarakai
soft drink ソフトドリンク sofuto dorinku
sole (fish) 鰈 karei
sole (shoe) 靴底 kutsuzoko
soluble 溶けやすい tokeyasui
some 幾らか ikuraka
someone, somebody 誰か dareka

ENGLISH → JAPANESE

something 何か nanika
sometimes 時々 tokidoki
somewhere どこかで dokokade
son 息子 musuko
son-in-law 義理の息子 giri no musuko
song 歌 uta
soon すぐに suguni
sore 苦 ku
sore, it's sore 痛い itai
sore throat 喉が痛い nodo ga itai
Sorry! ごめんなさい! gomennasai!
sort 種類 shurui
soup スープ supu
sour 酸っぱい suppai
south 南 minami
South Africa 南アフリカ minami afurika
South African 南アフリカ人 minami afurika jin
souvenir お土産 omiyage
spade 鍬 kuwa
Spain スペイン supein
Spaniard, Spanish スペイン人 supein jin
spanner スパナ supana
spare part スペアパーツ supea patsu
spare tyre スペアタイヤ supea taiya
spark plug スパークプラグ supaku puragu
sparkling スパークリング supakuringu
speak 話す hanasu
speciality 名物 meibutsu

spectacles 眼鏡 megane
speed 速度 sokudo
speed limit 制限速度 seigensokudo
speedometer 速度計 sokudokei
spell スペル superu
spend (money) 使う tsukau
spend (time) 費やす tsuiyasu
spice 香辛料 koshinryo
spider 蜘蛛 kumo
spill こぼす kobosu
spin-dryer 脱水機 dassuiki
spinach ほうれん草 horenso
spine 背骨 sebone
spirit (soul) 精神 seishin
spirits (drink) アルコール類 arukooru rui
splinter とげ toge
spoil 駄目にする dameni suru
spoke (of wheel) スポーク supoke
sponge スポンジ supongi
sponge cake スポンジケーキ supongi keki
spoon スプーン supun
sprain (n) 捻挫 nenza
sprain (vb) 捻挫する nenza suru
spring (season) 春 haru
square 正方形 seihokei
stadium スタジアム sutajiamu
stain 染み shimi
stairs 階段 kaidan
stale 古い furui
stall 売店 baiten
stamp 切手 kitte

STA   SUB

staple (n, food) 主食 shushoku
staple (n) ホッチキスの芯 hocchikisu no shin
star 星 hoshi
start 出発 shuppatsu
starter (car) スターター sutata
station 駅 eki
stationer's 文房具店 bunboguten
stationery 文房具 bunbogu
statue 像 zo
stay 滞在 taizai
steal 盗む nusumu
steam スチーム suchimu
steep 急な kyuna
steer 舵を取る kaji wo toru
steering wheel ステアリングホイール sutearingu hoiru
step 段 dan
stepfather 義父 gifu
stepmother 義母 gibo
stew シチュー shichu
stick 棒 bo
sticking plaster 絆創膏 bansoko
still (yet) まだ mada
still (quiet) 静かな shizukana
sting (n) 針 hari
sting (vb) 刺す sasu
stitch 縫う nuu
stock (soup) だし dashi
stocking ストッキング sutokkingu
stolen 盗まれた nusumareta
stomach 胃 i

stomachache 胃痛 itsuu
stone 石 ishi
stop 止まる tomaru
stop sign 停止サイン teishi sain
stopover 立ち寄る tachiyoru
store (n) 店 mise
store (vb) 蓄える takuwaeru
storey 階 kai
storm 嵐 arashi
straight まっすぐ massugu
straight on まっすぐに massuguni
straightaway すぐに suguni
strange おかしな okashina
strange, stranger 見知らぬ人 mishiranu hito
strap 革紐 kawahimo
straw わら wara
strawberry イチゴ ichigo
stream 小川 ogawa
street 道 michi
street map 道路地図 doro chizu
strike 打つ utsu
string 紐 himo
striped 縞の shimano
stroke 発作 hossa
strong 強い tsuyoi
stuck 行き詰まる ikizumaru
student 学生 gakusei
student discount 学生割引 gakusei waribiki
stuffed 詰まった tsumatta
stupid 馬鹿 baka
subtitle 副題 fukudai
suburb 郊外 kogai

131

ENGLISH → JAPANESE

subway 地下鉄 chikatetsu
suddenly 突然 totsuzen
suede スエード suedo
sugar 砂糖 sato
sugar-free 砂糖なし sato nashi
suit スーツ sutsu
suitcase スーツケース sutsu kesu
summer 夏 natsu
summit 頂上 chojo
sun 太陽 taiyo
sunblock 日焼け止め hiyakedome
sunburn 日焼け hiyake
Sunday 日曜日 nichiyobi
sunglasses サングラス sangurasu
sunny 天気の良い tenki no yoi
sunrise 日の出 hinode
sunroof サンルーフ sanrufu
sunset 日没 nichibotsu
sunshade 日よけ hiyoke
sunshine 日光 nikko
sunstroke 日射病 nisshabyo
suntan 日焼け hiyake
suntan lotion 日焼けローション hiyake roshon
supper 夕食 yushoku
supplement 補助 hojo
sure 確か tashika
surfboard サーフボード safubodo
surgery (doctor's rooms) 外科 geka
surgery (procedure) 手術 shujyutsu

surname 苗字 myoji
surrounded 囲まれた kakomareta
suspension 一時停止 ichijiteishi
swallow 飲み込む nomikomu
swear (an oath) 誓う chikau
swear (curse) ののしる nonoshiru
swear word ののしり言葉 nonoshiri kotoba
sweat (n) 汗 ase
sweat (vb) 汗をかく ase wo kaku
sweater セーター seta
Sweden スウェーデン suweden
Swedish, Swede スウェーデン人 suweden jin
sweet 甘い amai
swell 腫れる hareru
swelling 腫れている hareteiru
swim 泳ぐ oyogu
swimming costume 水着 mizugi
swing 揺れる yureru
Swiss スイス人 suisu jin
Swiss-German ドイツ系スイス人 doitsu kei suisu jin
switch スイッチ suicchi
switch off 消す kesu
switch on つける tsukeru
Switzerland スイス suisu
swollen 腫れた hareru
synagogue シナゴーグ shinagogu

T

table テーブル teburu
table wine テーブルワイン teburu wain
tablecloth テーブルクロス teburu curosu
tablespoon テーブルスプーン teburu supun
tailor テーラー tera
take 取る toru
take-away food 持ち帰り用料理 mochikaeriyo ryori
talcum powder タルカムパウダー tarukamu pauda
talk 話す hanasu
tall 背の高い senotakai
tampon タンポン tampon
tangerine みかん mikan
tank タンク tanku
tape テープ tepu
tape measure 巻尺 makijyaku
tape recorder テープレコーダー tepu rekoda
taste 味 aji
tax 税 zei
taxi タクシー takushi
taxi driver タクシー運転手 takushi untenshu
taxi rank タクシー乗り場 takushi noriba
tea お茶 ocha
tea bag ティーバッグ ti baggu
teach 教える oshieru
teacher 先生 sensei
team チーム chimu
teapot ティーポット tipotto
tear (n) 涙 namida
tear (vb) 破る yaburu
teaspoon ティースプーン tisupun
teat (bottle) 乳頭 nyuto
teeth 歯 ha
telephone 電話機 denwaki
telephone call 電話 denwa
telephone directory 電話帳 denwa cho
television テレビ terebi
tell 言う iu
temperature 温度 ondo
temple 寺 tera
temporary 一時的な ichijitekina
tendon 腱 ken
tennis テニス tenisu
tennis court テニスコート tenisu koto
tennis racket テニスラケット tenisu raketto
tent テント tento
tent peg テント用ペグ tento yo pegu
terminal ターミナル taminaru
thank 感謝 kansha
that あれ are
the その sono
theatre 劇場 gekijyo
theft 泥棒 dorobo
there そこに sokoni
thermometer 温度計 ondokei
they 彼ら karera

thick 厚い atsui
thief 泥棒 dorobo
thigh 腿 momo
thin 痩せた yaseta
thing もの mono
think 考える kangaeru
third-party insurance 第三者保険 daisansha hoken
thirsty 喉が渇く nodo ga kawaku
this これ kore
this morning 今朝 kesa
this way こちら kochira
this week 今週 konshu
thorn 棘 toge
those あれら arera
thousand 千 sen
thread より糸 yoriito
throat 喉 nodo
throat lozenges のどあめ nodoame
through 通って totte
throw 投げる nageru
thumb 親指 oyayubi
thunder 雷 kaminari
thunderstorm 雷雨 raiu
Thursday 木曜日 mokuyobi
ticket 切符 kippu
ticket collector 改札係 kaisatsugakari
ticket office チケットオフィス chiketto ofisu
tide, low tide, high tide 潮、干潮、満潮 shio, kancho, mancho
tie 結ぶ musubu
tight きつい kitsui
tights タイツ taitsu (tights)

till (cash register) レジ reji
till (until) 〜まで ...made
time 時間 jikan
timetable 時刻表 jikokuhyo
tin 缶 kan
tin opener 缶きり kankiri
tinfoil アルミ箔 arumihaku
tiny 小さい chisai
tip 先 saki
tired 疲れた tsukareta
tissue ティッシュ tisshu
to 〜へ ...e
toad ヒキガエル hikigaeru
today 今日 kyo
toe 爪先 tsumasaki
together 一緒に isshoni
toilet トイレ toire
tolerate 耐える taeru
toll, toll road 有料道路 yuryodoro
tomato トマト tomato
tomato juice トマトジュース tomato jusu (juice)
tomorrow 明日 ashita
tomorrow morning/ afternoon/evening 明日の朝／午後／夕方 ashitano asa / gogo / yugata
tongue 舌 shita
tonight 今夜 konya
tonsillitis 扁桃炎 hentoen
too 〜も mo
too much 過度の kadono
tool 道具 dogu
toolkit 工具一式 koguisshiki
tooth 歯 ha
toothache 歯痛 haita

toothbrush 歯ブラシ haburashi
toothpick 楊枝 yoji
top トップ toppu
top floor 最上階 saijyokai
topless トップレス toppuresu
torch 懐中電灯 kaichudento
torn 破れている yabureteiru
total 合計 gokei
tough タフ tafu (tough)
tour 観光 kanko
tour guide 観光ガイド kanko gaido
tour operator ツアーオペレーター tsua opereta
tow 引く hiku
towel タオル taoru
tower タワー tawa
town 町 machi
town hall 市役所 shiyakusho
toy オモチャ omocha
tracksuit トレーニングウエア toreningu uea
traffic 交通 kotsu
traffic jam 交通渋滞 kotsu jyutai
traffic light 信号 shingo
trailer トレーラー torera
train 電車 densha
tram トラム toramu
tranquillizer 鎮静剤 chinseizai
translate 翻訳する hon yaku suru
translation 翻訳 hon yaku

translator 翻訳者 hon yakusha
trash ごみ gomi
travel 旅行 ryoko
travel agent 旅行代理店 ryoko dairiten
travel documents 渡航書類 toko shorui
travel sickness 乗り物酔い norimonoyoi
traveller's cheque トラベラーズチェック toraberazu chekku
tray トレイ torei
tree 木 ki
trolley トロリー torori
trouble 問題 mondai
trousers ズボン zubon
trout 鱒 masu
truck トラック torakku
true 本当 honto
trunk (of car) トランク toranku
try 試す tamesu
try on 試着する shichaku suru
tube チューブ chubu
tuna マグロ maguro
tunnel トンネル tonneru
turkey 七面鳥 shichimencho
Turkey トルコ toruko
Turkish, Turk トルコ人 toruko jin
turn 曲がる magaru
turn around 回す mawasu
turn off 消す kesu
turquoise トルコ石 toruko ishi

tweezers ピンセット
pin setto
twice 2度 nido
twin beds ツインベッド
tsuin beddo
twins 双子 futago
type タイプ taipu
typical 典型的な
tenkeitekina
tyre タイヤ taiya
tyre pressure
タイヤの圧力
taiya no atsuryoku

U
ugly 醜い minikui
ulcer 潰瘍 kaiyo
umbrella 傘 kasa
uncle 叔父 oji
uncomfortable
心地が悪い
kokochiga warui
unconscious 意識不明
ishikifumei
under 下 shita
underdone 生焼け
namayake
underground 地下 chika
underground (subway)
地下鉄 chikatetsu
underpants ズボン下
zubon shita
understand 理解する
rikai suru
underwear 下着 shitagi
unemployed 失業者
shitsugyosha
United Kingdom イギリス
igirisu

United States
アメリカ合衆国
amerika gasshukoku
university 大学 daigaku
unleaded petrol
無鉛ガソリン muen gasorin
unlimited 無制限 museigen
unlock 鍵を開ける
kagi wo akeru
unpack 荷物を出す
nimotsu wo dasu
unscrew ねじってはずす
nejitte hazusu
until ～まで ...made
unusual 変わった kawatta
up 上へ ue e
up-market 高級な
kokyu na
upside down さかさま
sakasama
upstairs 上階 jyokai
urgent 緊急 kinkyu
us 私たち watashitachi
use 使う tsukau
useful 便利な benrina
usual いつもの itsumono
usually いつもは itsumowa

V
vacancy 空き aki
vacation 休暇 kyuka
vaccine ワクチン wakuchin
vacuum cleaner 掃除機
sojiki
valid 有効 yuko
valley 谷 tani
valuable 貴重品 kichohin
value 価値がある
kachi ga aru

valve バルブ barubu
van バン ban
VAT 付加価値税 fukakachizei
veal 子牛 koushi
vegetables 野菜 yasai
vegetarian ベジタリアン bejitarian
vehicle 車 kuruma
vein 血管 kekkan
vending machine 自動販売機 jido hanbaiki
venereal disease 性病 seibyo
very とても totemo
vest ベスト besuto
vet (veterinarian) 獣医 jyui
via 経由 keiyu
Vienna ウィーン uwin
view 眺め nagame
village 村 mura
vinegar 酢 su
vineyard ワイン畑 wain batake
violet スミレ sumire
virus ウィルス uwirusu
visa 査証 sasho
visit 訪問 homon
visiting hours 訪問時間 homon jikan
visitor 訪問者 homon sha
voice 声 koe
volcano 火山 kazan
voltage ボルト boruto
vomit 吐く haku
voucher バウチャー baucha

W
wage 給料 kyuryo
waist ウエスト uesuto
waistcoat ベスト besuto
wait 待つ matsu
waiter/waitress ウェイター / ウェイトレス uweita / uweitoresu
waiting room 待合室 machiai shitsu
wake up 起きる okiru
wake-up call モーニングコール moningu koru
Wales ウェールズ uweruzu
walk 歩く aruku
wall 壁 kabe
wallet 財布 saifu
walnut くるみ kurumi
want ～が欲しい ...ga hoshii
war 戦争 senso
ward (hospital) 病棟 byoren
wardrobe 洋服ダンス yofukudansu
warehouse 倉庫 soko
warm 暖かい atatakai
wash 洗う arau
washbasin 洗面台 senmendai
washing powder 粉石鹸 konasekken
washing-up liquid 食器用洗剤 shokkiyo senzai
wasp スズメバチ suzumebachi
waste 無駄にする muda ni suru
waste bin ゴミ箱 gomi bako

watch (vb) 見る miru
watch (n) 腕時計 udedokei
watch strap 腕時計のベルト udedokei no beruto
water 水 mizu
watermelon スイカ suika
waterproof 防水 bosui
water-skiing 水上スキー suijyo suki
wave 波 nami
we 私たち watashitachi
weak 弱い yowai
wear 着る kiru
weather 天気 tenki
weather forecast 天気予報 tenkiyoho
web ウェブ uweb
wedding 結婚式 kekkonshiki
wedding present 結婚祝いの品 kekkoniwai no shina
wedding ring 結婚指輪 kekkon yubiwa
Wednesday 水曜日 suiyobi
week – last week, this week, next week, a week ago 週 — 先週、今週 来週、1週 間前 shu – sen shu, konshu, raishu, iss ukanmae
weekday 平日 heijitsu
weekend 週末 shumatsu
weekly 毎週 maishu
weigh 重さを計る omosa wo hakaru
weight 重量 jyuryo
weird 変わった kawatta
welcome 歓迎 kangei

well 良い yoi
Welsh, Welshman, Welshwoman ウェールズ、ウェールズ人男性、ウェールズ人女性 uweruzu, uweruzujin dansei, uweru zujin jyosei
were 〜であった。...deatta
west 西 nishi
wet 濡れる nureru
wetsuit ウェットスーツ uettosutsu
What? 何? nani?
What is wrong? どうしましたか? doshimashitaka?
What's the matter? どうしましたか? doshimashitaka?
What's the time? 何時ですか? nanji desuka?
wheel 車輪 sharin
wheel clamp 車輪止め sharin dome
wheelchair 車椅子 kurumaisu
When? いつ? itsu?
Where? どこ? doko?
Which? どちら? dochira?
while 〜の間に ...no aida ni
whipped cream ホイップクリーム hoippu kurimu
white 白 shiro
Who? 誰? dare?
whole (n) 全部 zenbu
whole (adj) 完全な kanzenna
wholemeal bread 全麦パン zenmugi pan

領 収 書		
車番・チケット・クーポン・割引		No.3910
日付	2015年04月28日	
車番	1007	0000
乗務員		
		¥780円

領収 ¥780円

上記の様に領収致しました
毎度ご乗車ありがとうございます。

K.Y.K TAXI
関西個人京都四条グループ一匹会所属
TEL (075) 661-2244

Whose? 誰の? dareno?
Why? なぜ? naze?
wide 幅が広い haba ga hiroi
widower, widow
　男やもめ、未亡人
　otoko yamome, miboujin
wife 妻 tsuma
wig かつら katsura
win 勝つ katsu
wind 風 kaze
window 窓 mado
window seat 窓側の席
　madogawa no seki
windscreen フロントグラス
　furonto gurasu
windscreen wiper
　フロントグラスワイパー
　furonto gurasu waipa
windy 風が強い
　kaze ga tsuyoi
wine ワイン wain
wine glass ワイングラス
　wain gurasu
winter 冬 fuyu
wire ワイヤー waiya
wish 望む nozomu
with 〜と共に ...to tomoni
without 〜なしに ...nashi ni
witness 目撃者
　mokugekisha
wolf 狼 okami
woman 女 onna
wood 木 ki
wool ウール uru
word 言葉 kotoba
work 仕事 shigoto
world 世界 sekai
worried 心配する
　shinpai suru
worse もっと悪い
　motto warui
worth 価値 kachi
wrap up 包む tsutsumu
wrapping paper
　ラッピングペーパー
　rappingu pepa
wrinkles 皺 shiwa
wrist 手首 tekubi
write 書く kaku
writing paper 筆記用紙
　hikkiyoshi

X
X-ray レントゲン rentogen

Y
yacht ヨット yotto
year 年 toshi
yellow 黄色 kiiro
yellow pages
　イエローページ iero peji
yes はい hai
yesterday 昨日 kino
yolk 卵の黄身
　tamago no kimi
you あなた anata
young 若い wakai
your あなたの anatano
youth hostel
　ユースホステル
　yusu hosuteru

Z
zero ゼロ zero
zipper, zip fastener
　チャック chakku
zone ゾーン zon
zoo 動物園 dobutsu en

A

aamondo アーモンド almond
aamuchea アームチェア armchair
abara アバラ rib
aburakoi 脂っこい fatty
aburappoi 油っぽい greasy
adaputa アダプター adapter
adobaisu アドバイス advice
adobaisu suru アドバイスする advise
agaru 上がる get up
ageru 揚げる fry
ageru あげる give
ageta 揚げた fried
ago 顎 chin, jaw
agohige あごひげ beard
ahiru アヒル duck
ai 愛 love (n)
aidea アイデア idea
airon アイロン iron (appliance)
airon dai アイロン台 ironing board
airurando アイルランド Ireland
airurandojin, airu-dandojin dansei, airurandojin josei アイルランド人、アイルランド人男性、アイルランド人女性 Irish, Irishman/woman
aisatsu 挨拶 greeting
aishado アイシャドウ eye shadow
aisu kohi アイスコーヒー iced coffee
aisu kurimu アイスクリーム ice cream
aisu suketo アイススケート ice skates
aisuru 愛する love (vb)
aji 味 flavour, taste
aka 赤 red
aka wain 赤ワイン red wine
akarui 明るい light (colour)
akeru 開ける open
aki 秋 autumn
aki 空き vacancy
akusento アクセント accent
akuseru アクセル accelerator
ama gappa 雨合羽 raincoat
amai 甘い sweet
ame 飴 candy
ame 雨 rain
amemashite omedeto! あけましておめでとう。! Happy New Year!
amerika gasshukoku アメリカ合衆国 United States
ami 網 net
amibo 編み棒 knitting needle
amiyaki no 網焼きの grilled
amu 編む knit
ana 穴 hole
anata あなた you
anatano あなたの your
anba アンバー amber
anda mono 編んだもの plait
ansho bango 暗証番号 pin number
anzen 安全 safe (adj)

anzen beruto 安全ベルト life belt, safety belt
anzen herumetto 安全ヘルメット crash helmet
anzen pin 安全ピン safety pin
ao 青 blue
aojiroi 青白い pale
apato アパート apartment, block of flats
arai 粗い rough
arashi 嵐 storm
arau 洗う wash
are あれ it (indirect object), that
arera あれら those
ari 蟻 ant
aruite iku 歩いて行く go (on foot)
arukooru rui アルコール類 spirits (drink)
aruku 歩く walk
arumihaku アルミ箔 tinfoil
asa 朝 morning
asai 浅い shallow
asatsuki アサツキ chives
ase 汗 sweat (n)
ase wo kaku 汗をかく sweat (vb)
ashi 足 feet, foot
ashi 脚 leg
ashihire 足ヒレ flippers
ashikubi 足首 ankle
ashita 明日 tomorrow
ashitano asa 明日の朝 tomorrow morning
atama 頭 head
atarashi 新しい new
atatakai 暖かい warm
ATM ATM auto-teller, cash dispenser
ato 後 after
atode 後で afterwards, later
atsui 暑い hot
atsui 厚い thick
atsumeru 集める collect
atsuryoku 圧力 pressure
au 会う meet
auto doa アウトドア outdoors
awadatsu 泡立つ fizzy
awaiiro 淡い色 fair (hair colour)
ayamari 誤り fault
aza あざ bruise
azukarijyo 預かり所 cloakroom

B
baggu バッグ bag
bagi バギー buggy
baiku バイク motorbike
baipasu バイパス bypass (road)
baiten 売店 stall
baka 馬鹿 stupid
bakageta 馬鹿げた ridiculous, silly
baketsu バケツ bucket, pail
bakku pakku バックパック backpack
bakkugia バックギア reverse gear
bakkumira バックミラー rear-view mirror
bakuhatsu 爆発 explosion
bampa バンパー bumper
ban バン van
bansoko 絆創膏 plaster, sticking plaster

bara バラ rose (flower)
barubu バルブ valve
barukoni バルコニー
  balcony
baruto kai バルト海
  Baltic Sea
basho 場所 place
basu バス bus
basu tei バス停 bus stop
basuketto バスケット
  basket
bata バター butter
batteri gire バッテリー切れ
  flat battery
baucha バウチャー
  voucher
bebi fudo ベビーフード
  baby food
bebiika ベビーカー pram
beddo ベッド bed
beddo kaba ベッドカバー
  bedspread
beirifu ベイリーフ
  bay leaf
bejitarian ベジタリアン
  vegetarian
bekon ベーコン bacon
bempi de 便秘で
  constipated
bengoshi 弁護士
  lawyer
benri 便利 convenient
benrina 便利な useful
beru ベル bell
berugii ベルギー Belgium
berugii jin ベルギー人
  Belgian
beruto ベルト belt
besuto ベスト vest,
  waistcoat
bichi ビーチ beach
bijinesu ビジネス
  business

bijinesu patona
  ビジネスパートナー
  partner (business)
biniru bukuro ビニール袋
  plastic bag
biru ビール beer
bisuketto ビスケット
  biscuit
biyoshi 美容師 hairdresser
biyoshi no 美容師の
  hairdresser's
bo 棒 stick
bochi 墓地 cemetery
boi furendo ボーイフレンド
  boyfriend
bokoen 膀胱炎 cystitis
bokushi 牧師 priest
bonnetto ボンネット
  bonnet, hood (car)
bootsu ブーツ boots
boru ボール bowl
boru pen ボールペン
  ballpoint pen
boruto ボルト voltage
boshi 帽子 cap, hat
bosui 防水 waterproof
botan ボタン button
boto ボート boat
botoru ボトル bottle
botsuki kyandi
  棒つきキャンディー
  lollipop
bottakuri ぼったくり
  rip-off
bubun 部分 part, portion
budo 葡萄 grapes
bumpo 文法 grammar
bunbogu 文房具
  stationery
bunboguten 文房具店
  stationer's
bunsho 文章
  sentence (grammar)

burajya ブラジャー bra
burakkukarento ブラックカレント blackcurrant
burande ブランデー brandy
burando ブランド brand
burashi ブラシ brush
burausu ブラウス blouse
bureki ブレーキ brake
bureki eki ブレーキ液 brake fluid
bureki raito ブレーキライト brake light
buresuretto ブレスレット bracelet
burifu kesu ブリーフケース briefcase
burochi ブローチ brooch
buryusseru ブリュッセル Brussels
busho 部署 department
busshitsu 物質 material
buta 豚 pig
butaniku 豚肉 pork
byoin 病院 clinic, hospital
byoki 病気 disease, illness
byoki de 病気で ill
byoren 病棟 ward (hospital)
byuti saron ビューティサロン beauty salon

C
CD pureia CDプレイヤー CD player
chairo 茶色 brown
chairudoshito チャイルドシート child car seat
chakku チャック zipper, zip fastener
channeru チャンネル channel
chata furaito チャーターフライト charter flight
chea rifuto チェアリフト chair lift
chekku in チェックイン check in
chekku suru チェックする check
cheko kyowakoku チェコ共和国 Czech Republic
chesu チェス chess
chi 血 blood
chichi 父 father
chichukai 地中海 Mediterranean
chigai 違い difference
chigau 違う different
chiiki 地域 area
chijimu 縮む shrink
chika 地下 underground
chikai 近い near (adj)
chikaku ni 近くに nearby (adv)
chikaku no 近くの nearby (adj)
chikamichi 近道 short-cut
chikashitsu 地下室 basement, cellar
chikatetsu 地下鉄 subway, underground, metro
chikau 誓う swear (an oath)
chikazuku 近づく near (vb)
chiketto ofisu チケットオフィス ticket office
chiku 地区 district, region
chikyu 地球 earth
chimu チーム team

chinmoku 沈黙 silence
chinseizai 鎮静剤 tranquillizer
chintai 賃貸 lease (n)
chintai suru 賃貸する lease (vb), rent
chirashi チラシ leaflet
chiritori ちりとり dustpan
chisai 小さい small, tiny
chisei no aru 知性のある intelligent
chizu チーズ cheese
chizu 地図 map
cho 蝶 butterfly
cho nekutai 蝶ネクタイ bow tie
chodo ちょうど just (only)
chojo 頂上 summit
choka nimotsu 超過荷物 excess luggage
chokaku shogai no 聴覚障害の deaf
chokoreto チョコレート chocolate(s)
chokusetsu 直接 direct
chokyori denwa 長距離電話 long-distance call
chomiryo 調味料 seasoning
choppu チョップ chop
chorikigu 調理器具 cooking utensils
chosa 調査 investigation
choshoku 朝食 breakfast
choteisha 調停者 pacifier
choten 頂点 peak
chubu チューブ tube
chugoku 中国 China
chui bukai 注意深い careful

chuin gamu チューインガム chewing gum
chukan 中間 medium
chukara wain 中辛ワイン medium dry wine
chuko 中古 second-hand
chumon 注文 order (n)
chumon suru 注文する order (vb)
chuo yubinkyoku 中央郵便局 main post office
chusei no 中世の medieval
chusha 注射 injection
chusha meta 駐車メーター parking meter
chusha suru 駐車する park (vb)
chushaihan kippu 駐車違反切符 parking ticket
chushin 中心 middle
chushoku 昼食 lunch

D
daasu ダース dozen
daburu ダブル double
daburu beddo ダブルベッド double bed
daburu rumu ダブルルーム double room
dai shudoin 大修道院 abbey
daiamondo ダイアモンド diamond
daiaringu kodo ダイアリングコード dialling code
daiaru ダイアル dial
daidokoro 台所 kitchen
daietto ダイエット diet
daigaku 大学 university

daijin 大臣 minister
daijobu 大丈夫 all right
daikon 大根 radish
daiku 大工 carpenter
dainingu rumu ダイニングルーム dining room
dairiseki 大理石 marble
daisansha hoken 第三者保険 third-party insurance
daiseido 大聖堂 cathedral
dakeredomo ～だけれども although
dambo 暖房 heating
dameji ダメージ damage
dameni suru 駄目にする spoil
dan 段 step
danboru ダンボール cardboard
dansei 男性 male
danshi toire 男子トイレ gents' toilet
dansu ダンス dance
dare? 誰？ Who?
dareka 誰か anybody, someone, somebody
daremo ... nai 誰も～ない nobody
dareno? 誰の？ Whose?
dashi だし stock (soup)
dasshi men 脱脂綿 cotton wool
dassuiki 脱水機 spin-dryer
dato wakaru ～だと分かる recognize
de nai ～でない not, none
deatta ～であった。were
deguchi 出口 exit
deito デイト date (fruit)

dekinai できない。couldn't
dekki chea デッキチェア deck chair
denki 電気 electricity
denkigishi 電気技師 electrician
denkino 電気の electric
denkyu 電球 light bulb
denmaku デンマーク Denmark
densensei no 伝染性の infectious
densha 電車 train
denshi renji 電子レンジ microwave oven
denwa 電話 call (n), telephone call
denwa bango 電話番号 phone number
denwa cho 電話帳 telephone directory
denwa kokanshu 電話交換手 operator (phone)
denwa o kiru 電話を切る hang up (phone)
denwaki 電話機 telephone
depato デパート department store
desu ～です。am, are, is
dezaato デザート dessert
disuku ディスク disk
dizeru ディーゼル diesel
doa ドア door
doaberu ドアベル doorbell
doaman ドアマン doorman
dobutsu 動物 animal
dobutsu en 動物園 zoo
dochira? どちら？ Which?

dogu 道具 equipment, tool
doi 同意 agreement
doitsu ドイツ Germany
doitsu kei suisu jin ドイツ系スイス人 Swiss-German
doitsujin ドイツ人 German
doko? どこ? Where?
dokodemo どこでも everywhere
dokokade どこかで somewhere
doku 毒 poison
doku no aru 毒のある poisonous
dokutsu 洞窟 cave
donatsu ドーナツ doughnut
donoyonishite? どのようにして? How?
dorai kurina ドライクリーナー dry cleaner's
doraia ドライアー dryer
doraiyaa de kami wo kawakasu ドライヤーで髪を乾かす blow-dry
doreshingu ドレッシング dressing (salad)
doriru ドリル drill
doro 泥 mud
doro 道路 road
doro chizu 道路地図 road map, street map
doro hyoshiki 道路標識 road sign
doro koji 道路工事 road works
doro no ana 道路の穴 pothole

dorobo 泥棒 burglar, thief
dorobo 泥棒 theft
doryo 同僚 colleague
doshimashitaka? どうしましたか? What is wrong? What's the matter?
doyo bi 土曜日 Saturday

E
e 絵 drawing
e 〜へ to
eakon エアコン air conditioning
ebi 海老 prawn/shrimp
eiga 映画 cinema
eiga 映画 film, movie
eigo 英語 English (language)
eigyo tantosha 営業担当者 sales representative
eikoku 英国 Great Britain
eki 駅 station, railway station
ekonomi kurasu エコノミークラス economy class
emu sun M寸 medium sized
en 円 circle
encho 延長 extension
encho kodo 延長コード extension lead
enjin エンジン engine
enjin ki エンジンキー ignition key
enki suru 延期する postpone
enpitsu 鉛筆 pencil
enpo 遠方 far
ensho 炎症 inflammation
entotsu 煙突 chimney

epuron エプロン apron
era (error) エラー error
erabu 選ぶ choose
erebeta エレベーター lift, elevator
eri 襟 collar
eru 得る get
esa 餌 bait
esukareta エスカレーター escalator
esutonia エストニア Estonia

F
fairu ファイル file (folder)
fakusu ファックス fax
fan beruto ファンベルト fanbelt
fasuto kurasu ファーストクラス first class
fenda フェンダー fender
fensu フェンス fence
feri フェリー ferry
firuta フィルター filter
foku フォーク fork
fomaru フォーマル formal
fuben 不便 inconvenience
fudosanya 不動産屋 estate agent
fuhaibutsu 腐敗物 septic
fuirumu フイルム film, negative
fujin fuku 婦人服 ladies' wear
fukai 深い deep
fukaina 不快な revolting
fukakachizei 付加価値税 VAT
fukano 不可能 impossible
fukin ふきん duster

fukkatsusai 復活際 Easter
fuku 服 clothes
fukudai 副題 subtitle
fukuramu 膨らむ inflate
fukuro ふくろう owl
fumikiri 踏切 level crossing
fuminsho 不眠症 insomnia
fun 分 minute
funatabi 船旅 boat trip
funayoi 船酔い seasick
fune 船 ship
funsui 噴水 fountain
furaipan フライパン pan, frying pan
furaito フライト flight
furanneru フランネル flannel
furansu フランス France
furansujin, furansujin dan sei, furansujin jyosei フランス人、フランス人男性、フランス人女性 French, Frenchman/woman
furasuko bin フラスコ瓶 flask
furemu フレーム frame
furenchi furai フレンチフライ French fries
furi o suru 振りをする fake (vb)
furonto gurasu フロントグラス windscreen
furonto gurasu waipa フロントグラスワイパー windscreen wiper
furu 振る shake
furui ふるい sieve
furui 古い stale, old
furutsu jyusu フルーツジュース fruit juice

fushin 風疹 German measles, rubella
futa 蓋 lid
futago 双子 twins
futo 封筒 envelope
futo 埠頭 quay
futon 布団 duvet
futon kaba 布団カバー duvet cover
futotte iru 太っている fat
futsuka yoi 二日酔い hangover
fuyu 冬 winter

G

ga 蛾 moth
ga hoshii 〜が欲しい want
ga okoru 〜が起こる happen
gacho ガチョウ goose
gaido ガイド guide
gaido boku ガイドブック guide book
gaido tsuki tsua ガイド付きツアー guided tour
gaikan 外観 façade
gaikoku no 外国の foreign
gaikokujin 外国人 foreigner
gaiyo 概要 general
gake 崖 cliff
gakkari suru がっかりする disappointed
gakko 学校 school
gakubuchi 額縁 picture frame
gakui 学位 degree (qualification)
gakusei 学生 student
gakusei waribiki 学生割引 student discount
gan 癌 cancer
ganbatte 頑張って good luck
gankai 眼科医 ophthalmologist
gareji ガレージ garage
garon ガロン gallon
garu furendo ガールフレンド girlfriend
gasorin ガソリン petrol
gasorin kan ガソリン缶 petrol can
gasorin sutando ガソリンスタンド petrol station
gasu ガス gas
gasu kukaa ガスクッカー gas cooker
gaun ガウン dressing gown
gei ba ゲイバー gay bar
geijutsu 芸術 art
geijutsuka 芸術家 artist
geka 外科 surgery (doctor's rooms)
geki 劇 play (n)
gekijyo 劇場 theatre
gekitotsu suru 激突する crash
gemu ゲーム game
gengo 言語 language
genkan 玄関 hall
genki desuka? 元気ですか? How are you?
genki na 元気な lively
genkin 現金 cash
genko 原稿 draught
genzai 現在 present (adj)

genzo shori 現像処理 film processing
geri 下痢 diarrhoea
gesui kan 下水管 drain
gesuto hausu ゲストハウス guesthouse
geto ゲート gate
getsuyo 月曜日 Monday
gezai 下剤 laxative
gia ギア gear
gia bokusu ギアボックス gearbox
gia reba ギアレバー gear lever
gibo 義母 stepmother
gifu 義父 stepfather
gifuto ギフト gift
gimu ジム gym
gin 銀 silver
giri no chichi 義理の父 father-in-law
giri no haha 義理の母 mother-in-law
giri no kyodai 義理の兄弟 brother-in-law
giri no musuko 義理の息子 son-in-law
giri no musume 義理の娘 daughter-in-law
giri no ryoshin 義理の両親 parents-in-law
giri no shimai 義理の姉妹 sister-in-law
girisha ギリシャ Greece
girisha jin ギリシャ人 Greek
gishi 技師 engineer
gitaa ギター guitar
go gatsu 5月 May
gogaku kosu 語学コース language course
gogo 午後 afternoon, p.m.
goguru ゴーグル goggles
gohan ご飯 meal
gokai 誤解 misunderstanding
gokan 強姦 rape (n)
gokan suru 強姦する rape (vb)
gokei 合計 total
gokiburi ゴキブリ cockroach
gomennasai! ごめんなさい! Sorry!
gomi ゴミ refuse (n), rubbish, litter
gomi ごみ trash
gomi bako ゴミ箱 waste bin
gomi no nagesute ゴミの投げ捨て litter (vb)
gomibako ゴミ箱 bin, dustbin
gomu ゴム rubber
gomuhimo ゴムひも elastic
gorufu jyo ゴルフ場 golf club (place)
gorufu kosu ゴルフコース golf course
gorufu kurabu ゴルフクラブ golf club (stick)
goshikku ゴシック Gothic
goto 強盗 break-in

goto ni au 強盗にあう mugged
gozen 午前 a.m. (before noon)
gunshu 群集 crowd
guramu グラム gram
gurupu グループ group
gyaku 逆 reverse (n)
gyarari ギャラリー gallery
gyuniku 牛肉 beef
gyunyu 牛乳 milk

H
ha 葉 leaf
ha 歯 tooth/teeth
haba ga hiroi 幅が広い wide
habu ハーブ herbs
habu ti ハーブティー herbal tea
haburashi 歯ブラシ toothbrush
hachi 蜂 bee
hachimitsu 蜂蜜 honey
hada 肌 skin
hado disuku ハードディスク hard disk
haha 母 mother
hai 肺 lung
hai はい yes
hai iro 灰色 grey
haikanko 配管工 plumber
hairu 入る enter
haisha 歯医者 dentist
haita 歯痛 toothache
haitatsu 配達 delivery
haitatsu suru 配達する deliver
haji 恥 shame
hajimemashite はじめまして How do you do? Pleased to meet you!
hakai suru 破壊する ruin
hakari 秤 scales
hakaru 測る measure (vb)
hakike 吐き気 nausea
hakka 発火 ignition
hakken suru 発見する discover
hako 箱 box
hakobu 運ぶ carry
haku 吐く vomit
hakubutsukan 博物館 museum
hamaki 葉巻 cigar
hambaga ハンバーガー hamburger
hamu ハム ham
hana 花 flower
hana 鼻 nose
hanasu 話す speak, talk
hanaya 花屋 florist
hanbai 販売 sale
hanbai in 販売員 salesperson
hanbun 半分 half (n)
hando baggu ハンドバッグ handbag
hando bureki ハンドブレーキ handbrake
handoru ハンドル handle
hanga ハンガー hanger, coat hanger
hangari ハンガリー Hungary
hangari jin ハンガリー人 Hungarian

hangu raidingu ハングライディング
hang-gliding
hankachi ハンカチ
handkerchief
hanketsu 判決
sentence (law)
hanma ハンマー
hammer
hansamu ハンサム
handsome
hantai 反対 opposite
hantai ni 反対に
against
hanto 半島 peninsula
hanzai 犯罪 crime
happi isuta!
ハッピーイースター!
Happy Easter!
harau 払う pay
hareru 腫れる swell
hareru 腫れた swollen
hareta 晴れた fine
(weather)
hareteiru 腫れている
swelling
haretsu suru 破裂する
burst
hari 針 needle, sting (n)
haru 春 spring (season)
hasami ハサミ scissors
hashi 橋 bridge
hashi 端 edge
hashigo はしご ladder
hashika はしか
measles
hashiru 走る run
hasshin on 発信音
dialling tone
haten suru 発展する
develop
hatondo ... nai
ほとんど〜ない hardly

hatsudenki 発電機
dynamo
hatsuon suru 発音する
pronounce
hausu wain ハウスワイン
house wine
hayai 早い fast
hayarino 流行の
fashionable
hazukashigariya
恥かしがりや shy
hea burashi ヘアブラシ
hairbrush
hea doraia ヘアドライヤー
hairdryer
hebi 蛇 snake
heddo fon ヘッドフォン
headphones
heddo raito ヘッドライト
headlight/s
heigen 平原 plain
heijitsu 平日 weekday
heikin 平均 average
heisa 閉鎖 blocked
heiten 閉店 closed
hen na 変な peculiar
henji 返事 answer (n)
henji suru 返事する
answer (vb)
henka suru 変化する
change (vb)
henkin 返金 refund (n)
henkin suru 返金する
refund (vb)
hento 返答 reply (n)
hento suru 返答する
reply (vb)
hentoen 扁桃炎
tonsillitis
henzutsu 偏頭痛
migraine
herasu 減らす
reduce

herikoputa ヘリコプター helicopter
herumetto ヘルメット helmet
herunia ヘルニア hernia
heya 部屋 room
hezerunattsu ヘーゼルナッツ hazelnut
hi 火 fire, light
hibi ひび fracture
hicchi haiku ヒッチハイク hitchhike
hidari, hidari ni 左, 左に left, to the left
hidari handoru 左ハンドル left-hand drive
hidari kiki 左利き left-handed
hidoi ひどい awful
higashi 東 east
hige ひげ moustache
hiita ヒーター heater
hiji 肘 elbow
hijyoguchi 非常口 fire exit, emergency exit
hika chushaki 皮下注射器 hypodermic needle
hikari 光 light (n)
hikaru 光る light (verb)
hikidashi 引き出し drawer
hikigaeru ヒキガエル toad
hikiniku ひき肉 minced meat
hikkaki kizu 引っかき傷 scratch (n)
hikkaku 引っかく scratch (vb)
hikkiyoshi 筆記用紙 writing paper
hikkosu 引っ越す move house
hikkuri kaesu 引っくり返す knock over
hikoki 飛行機 aeroplane, plane, craft
hiku 引く pull, tow
hikui 低い low
himo 紐 string
hinichi 日にち date (of year), day
hininyaku 避妊薬 contraceptive
hinode 日の出 sunrise
hinpan ni 頻繁に frequent, often
hire ヒレ fillet
hiroba 広場 field, playground
hisho 秘書 secretary
hisshu no 必修の compulsory
hitai 額 forehead
hito 人 man, men, person
hito katamari ひと塊 loaf
hitobito 人々 people
hitokire 一切れ piece
hitoride 独りで alone
hitoshii 等しい even (equal)
hitsuji 羊 lamb, sheep
hitsuyo 必要 necessary
hitsuyo desu 必要です need (vb)
hitsuyo to suru 必要とする require

hitsuyosei 必要性 need (n)
hiyake 日焼け sunburn, suntan
hiyake roshon 日焼けローション suntan lotion
hiyakedome 日焼け止め sunblock
hiyoke 日よけ blind (n), sunshade
hiza 膝 knee
hoba kurafuto ホバークラフト hovercraft
hocchikisu no shin ホッチキスの芯 staple (n, stationery)
hochoki 補聴器 hearing aid
hodo 歩道 pavement, sidewalk
hoeru ほえる bark
hogaku 方角 direction
hogo 保護 guard
hohoemu 微笑む smile
hoikuen 保育園 nursery school
hoippu kurimu ホイップクリーム whipped cream
hojyo 補助 supplement
hokai 崩壊 collapse
hokani nanimo nai 他に何もない nothing else
hokano 他の other
hoken 保険 insurance
hoki ほうき broom
hokkai 北海 North Sea
hokoku 報告 report (n)
hokoku suru 報告する report (vb)
hokori 埃 dust

hokori no nai 埃のない duty-free
homo ホモ gay
homo sekusharu ホモセクシャル homosexual
homon 訪問 visit
homon jikan 訪問時間 visiting hours
homon sha 訪問者 visitor
homu shikku ホームシック homesickness
hon 本 book
hon yaku 翻訳 translation
hon yaku suru 翻訳する translate
hon yakusha 翻訳者 translator
hone 骨 bone
honmono 本物 real
honmonono 本物の genuine
honto 本当 true
honto ni 本当に really
honya 本屋 bookshop
hoo ほお cheek
horenso ほうれん草 spinach
horitsu 法律 law
hoseki 宝石 jewellery
hosekiten 宝石店 jeweller's
hoshi 星 star
hoshitsuzai 保湿剤 moisturizer
hosho 保証 guarantee
hossa 発作 stroke
hosu ホース hose pipe
hosuteru ホステル hostel

hotai 包帯 dressing (bandage)
hotondo ほとんど almost, mostly
hotondono ほとんどの most
houtai 包帯 bandage
hyo 表 list
hyoga 氷河 glacier
hyogen 表現 description
hyohakuzai 漂白剤 bleach
hyoji 標示 sign
hyoshiki 標識 signpost
hyuzu ヒューズ fuse
hyuzu bokkusu ヒューズボックス fuse box

I

i 胃 stomach
ia fon イヤフォン earphones
Ia rIngu イアリング earrings
ibiki いびき snore
ichi 1 one
ichi gatsu 1月 January
ichi jikan okini 1時間おきに hourly
ichiba 市場 market
ichido 一度 once
ichigo イチゴ strawberry
ichijiteishi 一時停止 suspension
ichijitekina 一時的な temporary
ichimai 一枚 slice

ie 家 house, home
iero peji イエローページ yellow pages
ifuku 衣服 dress
igirisu イギリス England, United Kingdom
igirisu kaikyo イギリス海峡 English Channel
igirisujin, igirisujin dansei, igirisujin jyosei イギリス人、イギリス人男性、イギリス人女性 English, Englishman/woman
iie いいえ no
iiwake 言い訳 excuse
iji suru 維持する keep
ijiwaruna 意地悪な mean, nasty
ikizumaru 行き詰まる stuck
ikkai 1階 first floor, ground floor
iku 行く go
ikubun 幾分 half
ikura desuka? いくらですか? How much is it?
ikuraka 幾らか some
ikutsu hitsuyo desuka? いくつ必要ですか? How many?
ikutsukano いくつかの several
ima 今 now
inabikari 稲光 flash (of lightning)
inaka 田舎 countryside
inchi インチ inch
indo jin インド人 Indian

inki na 陰気な gloomy
inku インク ink
inna chubu インナーチューブ inner tube
inoru 祈る pray
inoshishi イノシシ boar
insatsu butsu 印刷物 printed matter
insatsu suru 印刷する print
inseki 姻戚 in-laws
inshurin (insulin) インシュリン insulin
insutanto kohi インスタントコーヒー instant coffee
intai shita 引退した retired
inu 犬 dog
ippai no いっぱいの full
ippo tsuko 一方通行 one-way street
iriguchi 入り口 entrance
iro 色 colour
irui 衣類 clothing
iryo hoken 医療保険 medical insurance
iseebi 伊勢海老 lobster
isha 医者 doctor
ishi 石 stone
ishiki 意識 conscious
ishikifumei 意識不明 unconscious
isogashi 忙しい busy
isogu 急ぐ hurry, rush
isoide 急いで quickly
iss ukanmae 1週間前 a week ago
isshoni 一緒に together
isu 椅子 chair

isuramu kyoto イスラム教徒 Muslim
isuta eggu イースターエッグ Easter egg
ita choko 板チョコ bar of chocolate
itai 痛い painful, sore
itami 痛み ache, pain
itamidome 痛み止め painkiller
itamu 痛む hurt
itaria イタリア Italy
itariago イタリア語 Italian (language)
itariajin イタリア人 Italian
ito yoji 糸ようじ dental floss
itoko いとこ cousin
itsu? いつ? When?
itsumo いつも always, every
itsumono いつもの usual
itsumowa いつもは usually
itsuu 胃痛 stomachache
iu 言う say, tell

J

jaketo ジャケット jacket
jakki ジャッキ jack (car)
jampa ジャンパー jumper
jampa sen ジャンパー線 jump leads
jampu ジャンプ jump (n)
jampu suru ジャンプする jump (vb)
jamu ジャム jam
jankushon ジャンクション junction

jido hanbaiki 自動販売機 vending machine
jiei 自営 self-employed
jikan 時間 hour, time
jiko 事故 accident
jikokuhyo 時刻表 timetable
jimen 地面 ground
jimoto 地元 local
jimusho 事務所 office
jinko 人口 population
jinko kokansetsu chikan shujyutsu 人工股関節置換手術 hip replacement
jinsei 人生 life
jinshu 人種 race (people)
jinushi 地主 landlady, landlord
jinzo 腎臓 kidney
jishaku 磁石 magnet
jishin 地震 earthquake
jisho 辞書 dictionary
jissen suru 実践する practice
jisuberi 地すべり landslide
jisui 自炊 self-catering
jitai 事態 matter
jitensha 自転車 bicycle
jitensha yo doro 自転車用道路 cycle track
jitsu 耳痛 earache
jiyukeiyakuno 自由契約の freelance
jiyuna 自由な free
jogingu ジョギング jog (n)
jogingu suru ジョギングする jog (vb)
ju gatsu 10月 October
junin 住人 resident
jya (jar) ジャー jar
jyagaimo 芋 potato
jyaji ジャージ jersey
jyoba 乗馬 horse riding
jyogi 定規 ruler (for measuring)
jyoho 譲歩 concession
jyoho 情報 information
jyojyoni 徐々に gradually
jyokai 上階 upstairs
jyokaso 浄化槽 septic tank
jyoken 条件 condition
jyoku ジョーク joke
jyokyaku 乗客 passenger
jyoo 女王 queen
jyosei 性 female
jyosei 女性 lady
jyoseiyo toire 女性用トイレ ladies' toilet
jyozai 錠剤 pill
jyozosho 醸造所 brewery
jyu 銃 gun
jyubun na 十分な enough
jyui 獣医 vet (veterinarian)
jyuichi gatsu 11月 November
jyukushita 熟した ripe
jyunebu ジュネーブ Geneva
jyuni gatsu 12月 December
jyuryo 重量 weight

jyusu ジュース juice
jyutan 絨毯 carpet, rug
jyuwaki 受話器 receiver (telephone)
jyuyo dearu 重要である essential
jyuyo na 重要な important

K

ka 蚊 mosquito
ka ... ka 〜か〜 either ... or
kaa feri カーフェリー car ferry
kaba chaji カバーチャージ cover charge
kabe 壁 wall
kachi 価値 worth
kachi ga aru 価値がある value
kadigan カーディガン cardigan
kado カード card
kado 角 corner
kadono 過度の too much
kaeru カエル frog
kaesu 返す give back
kafein nokino カフェイン抜きの decaffeinated
kafunsho 花粉症 hay fever
kafusu botan カフスボタン cufflinks
kagakuseni 化学繊維 man-made fibre
kagami 鏡 mirror
kage 影 shade
kagi 鍵 key
kagi 鍵 lock (n)

kagi wo akeru 鍵を開ける unlock
kagi wo shimeru 鍵を閉める lock (vb)
kagu 家具 furniture
kagutsuki 家具付き furnished
kai 階 floor (storey)
kaichudento 懐中電灯 torch, flashlight
kaidan 階段 stairs
kaigai 海外 abroad
kaigan 海岸 coast, shore, seaside
kaigankeibi 海岸警備 coastguard
kaigi 会議 conference
kaigun 海軍 navy
kaika 階下 downstairs
kaimono bukuro 買い物袋 carrier bag
kaimu 皆無 nothing
kaisatsugakari 改札係 ticket collector
kaisha 会社 company
kaiso 海藻 seaweed
kaiten jikan 開店時間 opening times
kaiwashu 会話集 phrase book
kaiyo 潰瘍 ulcer
kaizen suru 改善する improve
kaji 家事 housework
kaji 舵 rudder
kaji wo toru 舵を取る steer
kajyo seikyu 過剰請求 overcharge
kakato かかと heel
kake 賭け bet
kakitome 書留 registered mail

kako 過去 past
kakomareta 囲まれた surrounded
kaku 書く write
kakudai 拡大 enlargement
kakunin 確認 confirmation
kakunin suru 確認する confirm
kakureru 隠れる hide
kakuri sareta 隔離された secluded
kami 髪 hair
kami 紙 paper
kami napukin 紙ナプキン paper napkin, serviette
kaminari 雷 lightning, thunder
kamisama 神様 God
kamisori かみそり razor
kamisori no ha かみそりの刃 razor blade
kamo shirenai 〜かもしれない may, might
kamome かもめ seagull
kampai 乾杯 Cheers!
kamu 噛む bite
kan 缶 can, tin
kan i beddo 簡易ベッド cot
kan i daidokoro 簡易台所 kitchenette
kanada カナダ Canada
kanamono ya 金物屋 hardware shop, ironmonger's
kanari かなり fairly, quite
kanashii 悲しい sad
kancho 干潮 low tide
kandai 寛大 generous
kangaeru 考える think

kangei 歓迎 hail
kangei 歓迎 welcome
kangofu 看護婦 nurse
kani カニ crab
kanjiru 感じる feel
kanjya 患者 patient
kanjyo 勘定 bill
kanjyo doro 環状道路 ring road
kankaku 間隔 interval
kankiri 缶切り can opener, tin opener
kanko 観光 sightseeing, tour
kanko gaido 観光ガイド tour guide
kankyaku 観客 audience
kanojyo 彼女 her, she
kanou 可能 possible
kansen 感染 infection
kansha 感謝 thank
kansha suru 感謝する grateful
kantanna 簡単な easy
kanu カヌー canoe
kanzen 完全 perfect
kanzen ni 完全に completely
kanzenna 完全な whole (adj)
kanzo 肝臓 liver
kao 顔 face
kappuru カップル couple
kara 〜から from (origin), from (time)
kara eizo カラー映像 colour film
kara hanareta から離れた off
karada 身体 body
karada no fujiyu na 体の不自由な handicapped

karadano fujiyuna 体の不自由な disabled
karano 空の empty
kare 彼 he, him
kare ni 彼に to him
kare no 彼の his
karei 鰈 sole (fish)
karera 彼ら they
karifurawaa カリフラワー cauliflower
kariga aru 借りがある owe
karikari shita カリカリした crisps
kariru 借りる borrow, hire
karu 狩る hunt
karui 軽い light (weight)
kasa 傘 umbrella
kasetto カセット cassette
kashidashi 貸し出し let (hire)
kashikoi 賢い clever
kashu 歌手 singer
kasu 貸す lend
kasutado カスタード custard
kata 肩 shoulder
katachi 形 form (shape)
katamichi chiketto 片道チケット single ticket
katen カーテン curtain
katon カートン carton
katorikku カトリック Catholic
katsu 勝つ win
katsura かつら wig
kau 買う buy
kauchi カウチ couch
kaunta カウンター counter
kawa 皮 leather
kawa 川 river
kawahimo 革紐 strap
kawaii 可愛い pretty
kawaita 乾いた dry
kawatta 変わった unusual, weird
kayui かゆい itch (n)
kazan 火山 volcano
kaze 風邪 flu
kaze 風 wind
kaze ga tsuyoi 風が強い windy
kazoku 家族 family
kazu 数 number
keburuka ケーブルカー cable car, funicular
keeki ケーキ cake
keeki ya ケーキ屋 cake shop
kega 怪我 hurts, injury
kega suru 怪我する injured
kegawa 毛皮 fur
kegawa no koto 毛皮のコート fur coat
keiba 競馬 horse racing
keibiin 警備員 security guard
keijiban 掲示板 noticeboard
keikaku 計画 plan
keikennoaru 経験のある experienced
keiko 稽古 lesson
keimusho 刑務所 prison
keiren 痙攣 cramp
keisanki 計算機 calculator
keisatsu 警察 police
keisatsukan 警察官 policeman/woman
keisatsusho 警察署 police station

keishiki baranai 形式張らない informal
keisokuki 計測器 meter
keitai bebiibeddo 携帯ベビーベッド carry-cot
keitai denwa 携帯電話 mobile phone
keiyaku 契約 contract
keiyu 経由 via
keizai 経済 economy
keizoku suru 継続する continue
kekkan 欠陥 flaw
kekkan 血管 vein
kekkanga aru 欠陥がある faulty
kekkon shiteiru 結婚している married
kekkon yubiwa 結婚指輪 wedding ring
kekkoniwai no shina 結婚祝いの品 wedding present
kekkonshiki 結婚式 wedding
kemuri 煙 smoke (n)
ken 腱 tendon
ken eki 検疫 quarantine
kenko 健康 fit (healthy)
kenko na 健康な healthy
kenko shokuhin ten 健康食品店 health food shop
keru 蹴る kick
kesa 今朝 this morning
keshi ケシ poppy
keshiki 景色 scenery
kesho otoshi 化粧落とし eye make-up remover
kesu ケース case
kesu 消す switch off, turn off
ketsuatsu 血圧 blood pressure
kettei 決定 decision
ki 木 tree, wood
ki horuda キーホルダー key ring
ki no hayai 気の早い rash
kibun ga warui desu! 気分が悪いです! sick, I'm going to be sick!
kichohin 貴重品 valuable
kieru 消える disappear
kigaeshitsu 着替え室 changing room, fitting room
kigengire 期限切れ expire
kiiro 黄色 yellow
kikai 機械 machine
kikan 期間 period
kikanshien 気管支炎 bronchitis
kiken 危険 danger
kikenna 危険な dangerous
kiko 気候 climate
kiku 聞く hear
kiku 聴く listen
kimeru 決める decide
kimyo na 奇妙な odd (strange)
kin 金 gold
kin en 禁煙 non-smoking
kinenbi 記念日 anniversary

kinenhi 記念碑 monument
kingan 近眼 short-sighted
kini tomeru 気に留める note
kinishinaide kudasai 気にしないで下さい it doesn't matter
kinjirarete iru 禁じられている forbidden
kinjyo 近所 neighbour
kinko 金庫 safe (n)
kinkyu 緊急 urgent
kinkyuno 緊急の emergency
kinniku 筋肉 muscle
kino 昨日 yesterday
kinshi sareta 禁止された prohibited
kinu 絹 silk
kinyobi 金曜日 Friday
kinzoku 金属 metal
kiosuku キオスク kiosk
kippu 切符 ticket
kireaji no warui 切れ味の悪い blunt
kirei きれい clean (adj)
kiri 霧 fog, mist
kiro キロ kilo
kiroguramu キログラム kilogram
kiroku 記録 record (legal)
kirometa キロメーター kilometre
kiru 切る cut
kiru 着る wear
kiruto キルト quilt
kisetsu 季節 season

kishuku sha 寄宿舎 boarding house
kisu キス kiss (n)
kisu 奇数 odd (number)
kisu suru キスする kiss (vb)
kita 北 north
kita airurando 北アイルランド Northern Ireland
kitai suru 期待する expect
kitanai 汚い filthy
kitsuen suru 喫煙する smoke (vb)
kitsui きつい hard, tight
kitsune 狐 fox
kitte 切手 stamp, postage stamp
kizetsu 気絶 faint
kizuku 気づく realize
kobosu こぼす spill
kobu こぶ lump
kochi コーチ coach
kochira こちら this way
kodaino 古代の ancient
kodo コード code
kodomo 子供 child
koe 声 voice
koen 公園 park (n)
kofuna 古風な old-fashioned
kogai 郊外 outskirts, suburb
kogeki 攻撃 attack (n)
kogeki suru 攻撃する attack (vb)
kogireina こぎれいな posh
kogitte 小切手 cheque

kogittecho 小切手帳
cheque book
kogittekado 小切手カード
cheque card
kogu 漕ぐ row (vb)
koguisshiki 工具一式
toolkit
kohei 公平 just, fair
kohi コーヒー coffee
koin コイン coin
koin randori
コインランドリー
launderette,
laundromat
koini 故意に
deliberately
koiru コイル coil
(contraceptive)
koishi 小石 shingle
kojyo 工場 factory
kokai 航海 sail
kokakurui 甲殻類
shellfish
kokan suru 交換する
exchange
kokana 高価な
expensive
koketsuatsu 高血圧
high blood pressure
kokku コック cook (n),
chef
kokoa ココア cocoa
kokochi yoi
心地よい
comfortable
kokochiga warui
心地が悪い
uncomfortable
kokode ここで here,
over here
kokoku 広告
advertisement

kokonattsu ココナッツ
coconut
kokubin 航空便 airmail
kokuken 航空券
air ticket
kokumin 国民
national
kokunaino 国内の
domestic
kokusaiteki na
国際的な
international
kokuseki 国籍
nationality
kokyaku 顧客 client
kokyono 公共の public
kokyu na 高級な
up-market
kokyu suru 呼吸する
breathe
komaraseru 困らせる
annoy
kome 米 rice
komedi コメディ
comedy
komichi 小道 path,
footpath
komori 子守 nanny
kompyuta
コンピューター
computer
komugiko 小麦粉
flour
kon banwa こんばんは
good evening
kon nichiwa こんにちは
good afternoon,
good day
kona 粉 powder
kona miruku 粉ミルク
powdered milk
konaien 口内
mouth ulcer

konasekken 粉石鹸
soap powder,
washing powder
kondeiru 混んでいる
crowded
kondo 混同 mix-up
kondo suru 混同する
mix up
kondomu コンドーム
condom
konpasu コンパス
compass
konranshita 混乱した
confused
konsato コンサート
concert
konsento コンセント
plug (elec)
konshu 今週
this week
kontakuto renzu
コンタクトレンズ
contact lenses
kontakuto renzu no hozoneki
コンタクトレンズの保存液
soaking solution
konya 今夜 tonight
konyakusha 婚約者
fiancé, fiancée
konyakushiteiru
婚約している engaged (to be married)
konzatsu shita
混雑した
jammed
koosu コース course
kopi コピー copy,
photocopy
koppu コップ cup, glass
(tumbler)
kora コーラ Coke
kore これ it (subject), this

koreisha 高齢者
senior citizen
korekuto koru
コレクトコール
collect call,
reverse-charge call
kori 氷 ice
koron 口論 quarrel (n)
koron suru 口論する
quarrel (vb)
korosu 殺す kill
koruku sennuki
コルク栓抜き
corkscrew
kosa suru 交差する
cross (vb)
kosaten 交差点
crossroads,
intersection
koshinryo 香辛料
spice
kosho 故障 breakdown
(of car)
kosho コショウ pepper
(spice)
kosho chu 故障中 out of order
koshoshita ban
故障したバン
breakdown van
koshu denwa
公衆電話
payphone
koshu denwa bokkusu
公衆電話ボックス
phone booth
kosoku doro
高速道路
freeway, motorway
kosui 香水 perfume
kotakuzai 光沢剤
polish (n)

koto コート coat
kotoba 言葉 word
kotowaru 断る refuse (vb)
kotsu 交通 traffic
kotsu jyutai 交通渋滞 traffic jam
kotsujiko 交通事故 road accident
kotta 凍った frozen
koun nimo 幸運にも fortunately
koushi 子牛 calf, veal
kowai 怖い afraid, be afraid of
kowareru 壊れる break
kowareta 壊れた broken
kowareyasui 壊れやすい breakable
koza 口座 account
kozeni 小銭 change (coins)
kozui 洪水 flood
kozutsumi 小包 parcel, packet
ku 苦 sore
kubi 首 neck
kuchi 口 mouth
kuchibeni 口紅 lipstick
kudamono 果物 fruit
kudari zaka 下り坂 downhill
kufukuno 空腹の hungry
kugatsu 9月 September
kui くい peg
kuji くじ lot
kujyo 苦情 complaint
kujyo wo iu 苦情をいう complain
kukaku 区画 compartment
kuki 空気 air
kukka クッカー cooker
kukki クッキー cookie
kuko 空港 airport
kumade くま手 rake
kumo 雲 cloud
kumo 蜘蛛 spider
kuni 国 country
kura bokkusu クーラーボックス cool bag, cool box
kuracchi クラッチ clutch (car)
kurage くらげ jellyfish
kurai 暗い dark
kurakushon クラクション horn (car)
kurasu クラス class
kurejitto kado クレジットカード charge card, credit card
kurenjingu roshon クレンジングローション cleansing lotion
kuri 栗 chestnut
kuria クリア clear
kurikaesu 繰り返す repeat
kurimu クリーム cream
kurisuchan nemu クリスチャンネーム Christian name
kurisumasu クリスマス Christmas
kurisumasu ibu クリスマスイブ Christmas Eve

kuro 黒 black
kurosu クロス cross (n)
kurosu wado クロスワード crossword puzzle
kuru 来る come
kuruku コルク cork
kuruma 車 car, vehicle
kuruma de iku 車で行く go (by car)
kuruma no buhin 車の部品 car parts
kuruma no kagi 車の鍵 car keys
kurumaisu 車椅子 wheelchair
kurumi くるみ walnut
kurutta 狂った mad
kuruzu suru クルーズする cruise
kusa 草 grass
kusatta 腐った rotten
kushami くしゃみ sneeze
kushi くし comb (n)
kushi de toku くしでとく comb (vb)
kusshon クッション cushion
kusuri 薬 drug (medicine)
kutsu 靴 shoe
kutsuhimo 靴紐 shoelace
kutsushita 靴下 socks
kutsuzoko 靴底 sole (of shoe)
kuwa 鍬 spade
kyabetsu キャベツ cabbage
kyabin キャビン cabin
kyabureta キャブレター carburettor
kyakusha 客車 carriage
kyakushitsu gakari 客室係 chambermaid
kyanpu キャンプ camp
kyanpu jyo キャンプ場 camp site
kyanseru キャンセル cancellation
kyanseru suru キャンセルする cancel
kyaraban キャラバン caravan
kyaraban jyo キャラバン場 caravan site
kyo 今日 today
kyoka 許可 permit (n)
kyoka suru 許可する let, allow, permit (vb)
kyokai 教会 church
kyoken byo 狂犬病 rabies
kyoko sa 強固さ iron
kyori 距離 distance
kyoudai 兄弟 brother
kyoyu 共有 share
kyuden 宮殿 palace
kyujyo 救助 rescue (n)
kyujyo suru 救助する rescue (vb)
kyuka 休暇 vacation
kyukei suru 休憩する rest (relax)
kyuko 急行 express (train)
kyukon 球根 bulb (plant)
kyukyu byoren 救急病棟 casualty department

kyukyubako 救急箱 first-aid kit
kyukyusha 救急車 ambulance
kyumei doi 救命胴衣 life jacket
kyuna 急な steep
kyuri キュウリ cucumber
kyuryo 給料 wage
kyusei 旧姓 maiden name

M
mabushii まぶしい bright
macchi マッチ matches (for lighting)
machi 町 town
machiai shitsu 待合室 waiting room
machiwabiru 待ちわびる look forward to
mada まだ still (yet)
made ～まで till (until)
mado 窓 window
madogawa no seki 窓側の席 window seat
mae 前 front
maebarai 前払い advance, in advance
maekin 前金 deposit
mafura マフラー exhaust pipe
magaru 曲がる turn
mageru 曲げる bend
magomusuko 孫息子 grandson
magomusume 孫娘 granddaughter
magu マグ mug
maguro マグロ tuna

mai jikan no 毎時間の hourly
mainichi 毎日 daily
mairu マイル mile
maishu 毎週 weekly
maitoshi no 毎年の annual
maitsuki 毎月 monthly
makeru 負ける lose
makige no 巻き毛の curly
makijyaku 巻尺 tape measure
maku 巻く roll
makura 枕 pillow
makura kaba 枕カバー pillowcase
mamaredo マーマレード marmalade
mame 豆 bean, pea
mamorareta 守られた sheltered
manabu 学ぶ learn
mancho 満潮 high tide
mane beruto マネーベルト money belt
manejya マネージャー manager
manikyua eki マニキュア液 nail polish/varnish
manikyua otoshi マニキュア落とし nail polish remover
manyuaru マニュアル manual
marui 丸い round
mashu poteto マッシュポテト mashed potatoes

masshurumu マッシュルーム mushroom
massugu まっすぐ straight
massuguni まっすぐに straight on
masu 鱒 trout
masui 麻酔 anaesthetic
masukara マスカラ mascara
masuku マスク mask
masutado マスタード mustard
masuto マスト mast
mata また again
maton マトン mutton
matsu 待つ wait
matsubazue 松葉杖 crutches
matsuri 祭り fair (fête), festival
mattoresu マットレス mattress
mawarimichi 回り道 roundabout
mawasu 回す turn around
mayaku 麻薬 drug (narcotic)
mayonezu マヨネーズ mayonnaise
mayotta 迷った lost
mazushii 貧しい poor (impecunious)
me 目 eye
mega sameru 目が覚める awake
megane 眼鏡 glasses, spectacles

meganeya 眼鏡屋 optician
megusuri 目薬 eye drops
mei 姪 niece
meibutsu 名物 speciality
meido メイド maid
mein kosu メインコース main course
mein suicchi メインスイッチ mains switch
mekanikku メカニック mechanic
memaiga suru めまいがする dizzy
memocho メモ帳 notepaper
men 綿 cotton
menkyo 免許 licence
menyu メニュー menu
merenge メレンゲ meringue
meron メロン melon
messeji メッセージ message
metoru メートル metre
mettani nai めったにない rare
mibun shomeisho 身分証明書 identity card
michi 道 street
midiamu rea ミディアムレア medium rare (meat)
midori 緑 green
migaku 磨く polish (vb)
migi handoru 右ハンドル right-hand drive

mijikai 短い short
mikan みかん tangerine
mikkusu ミックス mix
mimi 耳 ear
mina 皆 everyone
minami 南 south
minami afurika 南アフリカ South Africa
minami afurika jin 南アフリカ人 South African
minato 港 harbour, port
mineraru uota ミネラルウォーター mineral water
mingei 民芸 folk
minikui 醜い ugly
minshuku 民宿 bed & breakfast
minto ミント mint
miru 見る see, watch (vb)
misa ミサ Mass (rel)
mise 店 shop, store (n)
miseru 見せる show (vb)
mishiranu hito 見知らぬ人 strange, stranger
mitasu 満たす fill, fill in, fill up
mitingu ミーティング meeting
mitsukaranai 見つからない missing
mitsukeru 見つける find
mizu 水 water
mizu umi 湖 lake
mizuboso 水疱瘡 chicken pox

mizubukure 水膨れ blister
mizugi 水着 swimming costume
mizuire 水入れ jug
mizukiri boru 水切りボール colander
mo 〜も too
mo mata 〜もまた also
mo sukoshide もう少しで nearly
mochikaeriyo ryori 持ち帰り用料理 take-away food
mochikomu 持ち込 bring in
mocho en 盲腸炎 appendicitis
modoru 戻る go back, return
modottekuru 戻ってくる come back
mofu 毛布 blanket
mohitotsu もう一つ another
mokugekisha 目撃者 witness
mokutekichi 目的地 destination
mokuyobi 木曜日 Thursday
momo 桃 peach
momo 腿 thigh
momoku 盲目 blind (adj)
mondai 問題 problem, trouble
moningu koru モーニングコール wake-up call

mono もの thing
monohoshiyo ropu 物干し用ロープ clothes line
moreru 漏れる leak (vb)
mori 森 forest
moshi もし if
moshi damenara もしだめなら if not
mosuku モスク mosque
mota モーター motor
mota boto モーターボート motorboat
motte kuru 持ってくる bring
motteiru 持っている have
motto もっと more
motto warui もっと悪い worse
motto yasui もっと安い cheaper
muda ni suru 無駄にする waste
muen 無鉛 lead-free
muen gasorin 無鉛ガソリン unleaded petrol
mugi 麦 oats
muko de 向こうで over there
muku むく peel (vb)
mune 胸 breast, chest
muneyake 胸焼 heartburn
mura 村 village
murasaki 紫 purple
muru gai ムール貝 mussel
museigen 無制限 unlimited
mushi 虫 insect
mushi atsui 蒸し暑い humid
mushi sasare 虫さされ insect bite
mushi yoke 虫除け insect repellent
mushimegane 虫眼鏡 magnifying glass
musubu 結ぶ tie
musuko 息子 son
musume 娘 daughter
muzukashii 難しい difficult
myoji 苗字 surname

N
nadare 雪崩 avalanche
nagai 長い long (adj)
nagame 眺め view
nagare 流れ current
nagashi 流し sink
nageru 投げる throw
naifu ナイフ knife
naifu, foku ナイフ、フォーク cutlery
naka ni hairu 中に入る come in
nakami 中身 filling (sandwich)
naku 泣く cry
nama 生 raw
nama biru 生ビール draught beer
namae 名前 name, first name

namakete iru 怠けている lazy
namari 鉛 lead (metal)
namayake 生焼け underdone
namba pureto ナンバープレート number plate
nami 波 wave
namida 涙 tear (n)
namihazureta 並外れた extraordinary
nandemo 何でも anything
nandesuka? 何ですか? Pardon?
nani? 何? What?
nanika 何か something
nanji desuka? 何時ですか? What's the time?
nankinjyo 南京錠 padlock
nanko 軟膏 ointment
napukin ナプキン napkin
nashi 梨 pear
nashi ni ～なしに without
natsu 夏 summer
natto ナット nut (for bolt)
nattsu ナッツ nut
naya 納屋 barn
naze? なぜ? Why?
nazenara なぜなら because
nebukuro 寝袋 sleeping bag
nedan 値段 price
nega ネガ negative (photo)
negai 願い hope

negau 願う long (vb)
negawakuba 願わくば hopefully
negi ねぎ leek
neibi buru ネイビーブルー navy blue
neji ねじ screw
nejimawashi ねじ回し screwdriver
nejitte hazusu ねじってはずす unscrew
nekkuresu ネックレス necklace
neko 猫 cat
nemui 眠い sleepy
nenryo 燃料 fuel
nenryokei 燃料計 fuel gauge
nenza 捻挫 sprain (n)
nenza suru 捻挫する sprain (vb)
netsu 熱 fever, heat
nezumi ねずみ mouse, rat
ni ～に at
ni shukan 2週間 fortnight
ni taeru ～に耐える put up with
ni tsuiteiku ～について行く follow
ni yotte ～によって by
niban 2番 second
nibui 鈍い dull
nicchu 日中 midday
nichibotsu 日没 sunset
nichiyo daikuten 日曜大工店 DIY shop
nichiyobi 日曜日 Sunday

nido 2度 twice
nigatsu 2月 February
nigeru 逃げる escape
nigiru 握る hold
nikka boka ニッカボッカー knickers
nikki 日記 diary
nikko 日光 sunshine
niku 肉 meat
nikujiru 肉汁 gravy
nikuya 肉屋 butcher
nimotsu 荷物 luggage
nimotsu wo dasu 荷物を出す unpack
ningyo 人形 doll
ningyogeki 人形劇 puppet show
ninjin にんじん carrot
ninniku にんにく garlic
ninnki no aru 人気のある popular
ninshin chuzetsu 妊娠中絶 abortion
ninshin shiteiru 妊娠している pregnant
nioi 匂い smell
nisemono 偽物 dummy, fake (n)
nishi 西 west
nisshabyo 日射病 sunstroke
nita 似た similar
nito 2等 second-class
nitsuki 〜につき per
nitto uea ニットウェア knitwear
niwa 庭 garden
niwatori 鶏 chicken
no 〜の of
no aida ni 〜の間に among, during, while
no dochirademo nai 〜のどちらでもない neither ... nor
no kawarini 〜の代わりに instead
no muko ni 〜の向こうに over
no nakani 〜の中に in, into
no sobani 〜のそばに beside
no tameni 〜のために because of, for
no ueni 〜の上に on
no ushironi 〜の後ろに behind
no yona 〜のような like, as
noberu 述べる mention
noboru 登る climb
nochi 農地 farm
nodo 喉 throat
nodo ga itai 喉が痛い sore throat
nodo ga kawaku 喉が渇く thirsty
nodoame のどあめ throat lozenges
noho 嚢胞 cyst
nojyo 農場 farmhouse
noka 農家 farmer
nokku suru ノックする knock
nokori 残り rest (remainder)
nokoru 残る remain
nomi ノミ flea

nomikomu 飲み込む
swallow
nomimizu 飲み水
drinking water
nomimono 飲み物
drink (n)
nomu 飲む drink (vb)
non arukoru
ノンアルコール
non-alcoholic
nonoshiri kotoba
ののしり言葉
swear word
nonoshiru ののしる
swear (curse)
nori 糊 glue
norimonoyoi
乗り物酔い
travel sickness
noritsugibin 乗継便
connecting flight
noru 乗る get on, ride
noruwe ノルウェー
Norway
noruwe jin
ノルウェー人
Norwegian
noshinto 脳震盪
concussion
noto ノート notebook
noyou 膿瘍 abscess
nozoku 除く exclude
nozomu 望む wish
nudo bichi
ヌードビーチ
nudist beach
numachi 沼地 marsh
nuno 布 cloth
nureru 濡れる wet
nusumareta 盗まれた
stolen
nusumu 盗む steal
nuu 縫う sew, stitch

nyuji rando, nyuji rando jin ニュージーランド, ニュージーランド人 New Zealand, New Zealander
nyujyoryo 入場料
admission fee, entrance fee
nyusu ニュース news
nyuto 乳頭 teat (bottle)

O
o fukumu 〜を含む
included
o hyogen suru
〜を表現する
describe
o kensa suru
〜を検査する
inspect
o koete 〜を越えて
beyond
o miru 〜を見る look at
o nozoite 〜を除いて
except
o sashihiku 〜を差し引く
deduct
oba 叔母 aunt
oba hito オーバーヒート
overheat
obaa san おばあさん
grandmother
oboeru 覚える
remember
obun オーブン oven
obun tainetsusei no
オーブン耐熱性の
ovenproof
ocha お茶 tea
ochiru 落ちる fall
odanhodo 横断歩道
pedestrian crossing
odorokubeki 驚くべき
astonishing

ofuku chiketto 往復チケット return ticket
ofuro お風呂 bath
ogawa 小川 stream
oh 王 king
oh dori 大通り main road
ohayo おはよう good morning
ohkii 大きい large
oi 甥 nephew
oinuku 追い抜く overtake
oiru オイル oil
oishi おいしい delicious
oji 叔父 uncle
ojii san おじいさん grandfather
okami 狼 wolf
okan 王冠 crown
okane お金 money
okashina おかしな strange
okesutora オーケストラ orchestra
okii 大きい big
okini irino お気に入りの favourite
okiru 起きる wake up
okisa 大きさ measure (n)
okke オッケー OK
okotte 怒って angry
oku オーク oak
oku 置く put
okunai 屋内 indoors
okunai puru 屋内プール indoor pool
okureru 遅れる delay
okuru 送る send
okyakusama お客様 customer, guest
okyu teate 応急手当 first aid
omedeto! おめでとう! Congratulations!
omisoka 大晦日 New Year's Eve
omiyage お土産 souvenir
omocha オモチャ toy
omoi 重い heavy
omosa wo hakaru 重さを計る weigh
omoshiroi おもしろい funny
omoshiroi 面白い interesting
omuretsu オムレツ omelette
omutsu オムツ diaper
onaji 同じ same
ondo 温度 temperature
ondokei 温度計 thermometer
ongakuka 音楽家 musician
onna 女 woman
onna no ko 女の子 girl
onsen 温泉 hot spring
oodori 大通り avenue
ooyoso おおよそ approximately
opera オペラ opera
opun chiketto オープンチケット open ticket
oranda オランダ Netherlands
orandajin, orandajin dansei, orandajin jyosei オランダ人、オランダ人男性、オランダ人女性 Dutch, Dutchman, Dutchwoman

orenji オレンジ orange
orenji jyusu オレンジジュース orange juice
oribu オリーブ olive
oribu oiru オリーブオイル olive oil
oriru 下りる get off
oroshita おろした grated
oru オール oar
osensareta 汚染された polluted
oshieru 教える teach
oshime おしめ nappy
oshiri お尻 hip
oshitsu no 王室の royal
oshu kyodotai 欧州共同体 EC
oshu rengo 欧州連合 EU
osoi 遅い slow
osoku 遅く late
osoroshii 恐ろしい dreadful
osu 押す push
otafuku kaze おたふく風邪 mumps
otan 黄疸 jaundice
otoko yamome, miboujin 男やもめ、未亡人 widower, widow
otona 大人 adult
otoshitamago 落とし卵 poached
otosu 落とす drop

otsuri wa irimasen! お釣りはいりません! Keep the change!
otto 夫 husband
oudanhodo 横断歩道 crossing
owari 終わり end
owaru 終わる finish
oyasumi おやす good night
oyayubi 親指 thumb
oyogu 泳ぐ swim
oyoso およそ roughly

P
pafomansu パフォーマンス performance
pai パイ pie
painappuru パイナップル pineapple
paipu パイプ pipe (plumbing, smoking)
pairotto パイロット pilot
pajama パジャマ pyjamas, nightdress
pakingu disuku パーキングディスク parking disc
pakkeji 包み package
pakkeji horide パッケージホリデー package holiday
pama wo kakeru パーマをかける perm
pan パン bread
panfuretto パンフレット brochure
pankeki パンケーキ pancake

panku パンク flat tyre
panku suru パンクする puncture
panti パンティー panties
pantisutokkingu パンティーストッキング pantyhose
pantsu パンツ pants
panya パン屋 bakery
pasu パス pass
pasu seigyo パス制御 pass control
patan パターン pattern
pati パーティー party (celebration)
patona パートナー partner (companion)
pedaru ペダル pedal
peji ページ page
pen ペン pen
pen furendo ペンフレンド penfriend
penchi ペンチ pliers
penki ペンキ paint (n)
penki nuri ペンキ塗り painting
penki wo nuru ペンキを塗る paint (vb)
pesumeka ペースメーカー pacemaker
pesutori ペストリー pastry
petto ペット pet
piano ピアノ piano
pikunikku ピクニック picnic
piman ピーマン pepper (vegetable)
pin ピン pin
pin setto ピンセット tweezers

pinattsu ピーナッツ peanut
pinku ピンク pink
poketto ポケット pocket
pondo ポンド pound
ponpu ポンプ pump
porando ポーランド Poland
porando jin ポーランド人 Pole, Polish
porutogaru ポルトガル Portugal
porutogaru jin ポルトガル人 Portuguese
posuta ポスター poster
posuto ポスト post (n)
posuto kado ポストカード postcard
pota ポーター porter
poteto chippusu ポテトチップス chips
poto wain ポートワイン port (wine)
potoreto ポートレート portrait
puraibeto プライベート private
puramu プラム plum
purasuchikku プラスチック plastic
purattofomu プラットホーム platform
purezento プレゼント present (n)
purin プリン pudding
puroguramu プログラム programme, program
purotesutanto プロテスタント Protestant

puru プール pool
puruoba プルオーバー pullover

R
raberu ラベル label
raga ラガー lager
raifu gado ライフガード lifeguard
raimu ライム lime
raimugi pan ライ麦パン rye bread
raion ライオン lion
raishu 来週 next week
raita ライター cigarette lighter
raiu 雷雨 thunderstorm
rajieta ラジエーター radiator
rajio ラジオ radio
raketto ラケット racket
rampu ランプ lamp
ramu shu ラム酒 rum
rappingu pepa ラッピングペーパー wrapping paper
ratobia ラトビア Latvia
raunji ラウンジ lounge
razuberi ラズベリー raspberry
reba レバー lever
reddokaranto レッドカラント redcurrant
rei 例 example, for example
reigi tadashi 礼儀正しい polite
reihaidou 礼拝堂 chapel
reisei 冷静 calm
reitoko 冷凍庫 freezer
reizoko 冷蔵庫 fridge

reizun レーズン raisin
reji レジ cash desk, cash register, till
reji gakari レジ係り cashier
rekishi 歴史 history
rekishijyo no 歴史上の historic
rekodo レコード record (music)
remon レモン lemon
remonedo レモネード lemonade
renga レンガ brick
renraku suru 連絡する contact
renshu suru 練習する practise
rentaka レンタカー car hire, hire car
rentiru レンティル lentil
rentogen レントゲン X-ray
renzu レンズ lens
reshipi レシピ recipe
resu レース lace
resu レース race (sport)
resu kosu レースコース race course
retasu レタス lettuce
reto レート rate (of exchange)
retsu 列 queue, row (n)
retsu ni narabu 列に並ぶ queue (vb)
rezubian レズビアン lesbian
ribingurumu リビングルーム living room
ribon リボン ribbon

rikai suru 理解する understand
rikon shiteiru 離婚している divorced
rikyuru リキュール liqueur
rinneru リンネル linen
ritoania リトアニア Lithuania
rittoru リットル litre
riyo dekiru 利用できる available
rizoto リゾート resort
robi ロビー lobby
roden 漏電 leak (n)
roka 廊下 corridor
rokka ロッカー locker
roku gatsu 6月 June
ropu ロープ rope
ropu wo maku ロープを巻く coil (rope)
rorei nenkinsha 老齢年金者 old-age pensioner
roru pan ロールパン bun
roshutsu 露出 exposure
rosoku ろうそく candle
rufurakku ルーフラック roof-rack
rukusenburugu ルクセンブルグ Luxembourg
ryo 量 amount, quantity
ryogaejo 両替所 bureau de change
ryoho 両方 both
ryojikan 領事館 consulate
ryoken 旅券 passport
ryokin 料金 charge, cost
ryoko 旅行 travel
ryoko dairiten 旅行代理店 travel agent
ryori 料理 cook (vb)
ryoshi 漁師 fishmonger's
ryoshin 両親 parents
ryoshusho 領収書 receipt
ryucho 流暢 fluent
ryumachi リウマチ rheumatism

S
sabaku 砂漠 desert
sabisu サービス service
sabisu ryo サービス料 service charge
sabita 錆びた rusty
sadoru サドル saddle
safubodo サーフボード surfboard
sagasu 探す look for
saibankan 裁判官 judge
saida サイダー cider
saido disshu サイドディッシュ side dish
saifu 財布 purse, wallet
saigai 災害 disaster
saigo 最後 last
saijyokai 最上階 top floor
saijyuden suru 再充電する recharge
saikin 最近 recently
saiko reto 最高レート peak rate
saikoro さいころ dice
saishoni 最初に first, at first
saizu サイズ size
sakana 魚 fish
sakasama さかさま upside down

sakasani suru 逆さにする reverse(vb)
sake 鮭 salmon
sakebi 叫び shout (n)
sakebu 叫ぶ shout (vb)
sakeru 避ける avoid
saki 先 tip
sakka サッカー football (soccer)
sakka no shiai サッカーの試合 football match
sakkyokuka 作曲家 composer
sakotsu 鎖骨 collarbone
sakurambo さくらんぼ cherry
sakuya 昨夜 last night
samatageru 〜を妨げる disturb
san 〜さん Miss, Mr, Mrs, Ms
san gatsu 3月 March
sanchuwa zai 酸中和剤 antacid
sandaru サンダル flip flops, sandals
sandoicchi サンドイッチ sandwich
sangaku kyujyo 山岳救助 mountain rescue
sangurasu サングラス sunglasses
sanka suru 参加する join
sanrufu サンルーフ sunroof
sansei 賛成 agree
sanshokutsuki 3食付き full board
sara 皿 plate

sarada サラダ salad
sarada doressingu サラダドレッシング salad dressing
saranrappu サランラップ cling film
saru 去る go away
sasho 査証 visa
sasu 刺す sting (vb)
sato 砂糖 sugar
sato nashi 砂糖なし sugar-free
sayonara さようなら goodbye
sebone 背骨 spine
secchaku teipu 接着テープ adhesive tape
sei kin yobi 聖金曜日 Good Friday
seibori セイボリー savoury
seibyo 性病 venereal disease
seifu 政府 government
scigensokudo 制限速度 speed limit
seihatsu 整髪 haircut
seihokei 正方形 square
seikakuna 正確な accurate
seikakuni 正確に exactly
seikatai 聖歌隊 choir
seiki 世紀 century
seikyusho 請求書 invoice
seimei hoken 生命保険 life insurance
seinengappi 生年月日 date of birth
seiringu セイリング sailing

seiriyo napukin 生理用ナプキン sanitary pads
seishin 精神 mind, spirit, soul
seito 政党 party (political)
sekai 世界 world
seki 咳 cough (n)
seki 席 seat
seki wo suru 咳をする cough (vb)
sekidome 咳止め cough mixture
sekimen 赤面 blusher
sekitan 石炭 coal
sekken 石鹸 soap
sekkusu セックス sex
semai 狭い narrow
sen 線 line
sen 栓 plug (bath)
sen 千 thousand
sen nuki 栓抜き bottle opener
sen shu 先週 last week
senaka 背中 back
senchi センチ centimetre
seni 繊維 fabric
senjoeki 清浄液 cleaning solution
senmendai 洗面台 washbasin
senmenjyo 洗面所 lavatory
senotakai 背の高い tall
senpuki 扇風機 fan
senryo 染料 dye (n)
sensei 先生 teacher
sensha 洗車 car wash
senso 戦争 war
senta センター centre
sentaku 洗濯 laundry

sentaku basami 洗濯ばさみ clothes peg
sentoraru hitingu セントラルヒーティング central heating
sentoraru rokkingu セントラルロッキング central locking
senzai 洗剤 detergent
serori セロリ celery
serufusabisu セルフサービス self-service
sesshi 摂氏 Centigrade
seta セーター sweater
setsudan sareta 切断された disconnected
setsugo 接合 joint
setsumei suru 説明する explain
setsuzoku 接続 connection (elec, phone)
setto 窃盗 burglary
setto menyu セットメニュー set menu
sewa suru 世話する look after
sewanin 世話人 caretaker
shakkin 借金 debts
shampen シャンペン champagne
shampu to setto シャンプーとセット shampoo and set
sharin 車輪 wheel
sharin dome 車輪止め wheel clamp
sharyo hoken 車両保険 car insurance

179

SHA　　　　　　　　　　　　　　　　　　　　SHI

shasen 車線 lane
shashin 写真 photo, photograph (n), picture
shashin wo toru 写真を撮る photograph (vb)
shatsu シャツ shirt
shatta シャッター shutter
shawa シャワー shower
shazai 謝罪 apology
shefu シェフ chef
shi 市 city
shiai 試合 match (sport)
shiai wo suru 試合をする play (vb)
shiawase 幸せ happy
shibo 死亡 death
shibo suru 死亡する die
shiboshita 死亡した dead
shichaku suru 試着する\ try on
shichi gatsu 7月 July
shichimencho 七面鳥 turkey
shichu シチュー stew
shigoto 仕事 job, work
shiharai 支払い payment
shiharaizumi no 支払済みの paid
shihonkin 資本金 capital (money)
shijiki 指示器 indicator
shikai 視界 sight
shikashi しかし but
shiken 試験 examination
shiki jaku 色弱 colour blind
shima 島 island
shimai 姉妹 sister
shimano 縞の striped

shimbun 新聞 newspaper
shimbun baiten 新聞売店 news stand
shimedasu 締め出す lock out
shimekiri 締め切り due
shimeru 締める fasten, shut
shimetta 湿った damp
shimi 染み stain
shimin 市民 citizen
shimo 霜 frost
shimpu 新婦 bride
shinagogu シナゴーグ synagogue
shinakereba naranai 〜しなければならない。 have to
shinakutewa naranai 〜しなくてはならない。 must
shindai 寝台 couchette
shindaisha 寝台車 sleeper, sleeping car
shingo 信号 traffic light
shinguru シングル single
shinguru beddo シングルベッド single bed
shingurusu シングルス shingles
shinjiru 信じる believe
shinjyu 真珠 pearl
shinken 真剣 serious
shinkon ryoko 新婚旅行 honeymoon
shinnen 新年 New Year
shinpai suru 心配する worried

shinro 新郎 bridegroom
shinsei na 神聖な holy
shinseki 親戚 relative, relation
shinsen 新鮮 fresh
shinsetsu na 親切な friendly, kind
shinsetsu na motenashi 親切なもてなし hospitality
shinshi fuku 紳士服 menswear
shinya 深夜 midnight
shinzo 心臓 heart
shinzo hossa 心臓発作 heart attack
shio 塩 salt
shio 潮 tide
shippai 失敗 mistake
shirafuno しらふの sober
shiro 城 castle
shiro 白 white
shishobako 私書箱 post office box
shita 下 bottom (at the), under
shita 舌 tongue
shitagi 下着 lingerie, underwear
shitai 〜したい itch (vb)
shite iidesuka? 〜していいですか? Could I?
shiten 支店 branch (office)
shitoberuto シートベルト seatbelt
shitoberuto o shimeru シートベルトを締める fasten seatbelt

shitsu 質 quality
shitsu ga warui 質が悪い poor (quality)
shitsu to makura kaba シーツと枕カバー bed linen
shitsugyosha 失業者 unemployed
shitsumon 質問 enquiry, question
shitte iru 知っている know
shitto shite 嫉妬して jealous
shiwa 皺 wrinkles
shiyakusho 市役所 town hall
shiyochu 使用中 engaged occupied (e.g. toilet)
shizen 自然 nature
shizen no 自然の natural
shizenkoen 自然公園 nature reserve
shizukana 静かな still (quiet)
shizukani 静かに quiet
sho ショー show (n)
sho uwindo ショーウィンドー shop window
shodokuzai 消毒剤 disinfectant
shohi 消費 expenses
shohin 賞品 prize
shohosen 処方箋 prescription
shojiki 正直 honest
shoka furyo 消化不良 indigestion
shokai suru 紹介する introduce
shokaki 消火器 fire extinguisher

shoki de nai 正気でない
crazy
shokki 食器 crockery, dish
shokki araiki 食器洗い機
dishwasher
shokkiyo senzai 食器用洗剤
washing-up liquid
shokkiyo taoru 食器用タオル
dishtowel
shokku abuzoba ショック　アブゾーバ
shock absorber
shokuchudoku 食中毒
food poisoning
shokudosha 食堂車
buffet car
shokugyo 職業
occupation
shokuhinten 食品店
food shop
shokuryo wo ataeru 食料を与える feed
shomei 署名
signature
shomeisho 証明書
certificate
shomikigen 賞味期限
sell-by date
shonen 少年 boy
shoppingu senta ショッピングセンター
shopping centre
shorai 将来 future
shorui 書類 document
shosai 詳細 details
shosetsu 小説 novel
shoshinsha 初心者
beginner

shoshinshayo no gerende 初心者用のゲレンデ
nursery slope
shotai 招待 invitation
shotai suru 招待する
invite
shotsu ショーツ shorts
shoubotai 消防隊
fire brigade
shoyusha 所有者
owner
shu 週 week
shuccho 出張
business trip
shucho suru 主張する
insist
shudoin 修道院
monastery
shujyutsu 手術
surgery (procedure)
shukaku 収穫 harvest
shukan 習慣 custom
shuki 周期 cycle
shukketsu 出血 bleed
shukuhaku 宿泊
accommodation
shukujitsu 祝日
public holiday
shukusho 縮小
reduction
shukuya 宿屋 inn
shumatsu 週末
weekend
shunkan 瞬間 moment
shuppatsu 出発
departure, start
shuppatsu raunji 出発ラウンジ
departure lounge
shuppatsu suru 出発する
depart

shuri 修理 repair (n)
shuri suru 修理する fix, repair (vb)
shurui 種類 sort
shuryo menkyo 狩猟免許 hunting permit
shusho 首相 prime minister
shushoku 主食 staple (n, food)
shussei 出生 birth
shussei shomeisho 出生証明書 birth certificate
shuto 首都 capital (city)
shuyo na 主要な main
shuyu 周遊 excursion
shuzen 修繕 mend
sigunaru シグナル signal
singuru rumu シングルルーム single room
so ireba 総入れ歯 dentures
so on 騒音 noise
soda ソーダ soda
sodaina 壮大な grand
sode nakereba そうでなければ otherwise
sofubo 祖父母 grandparents
sofuto dorinku ソフトドリンク soft drink
sogankyo 双眼鏡 binoculars
soji suru 掃除する clean (vb)
sojiki 掃除機 vacuum cleaner
soketto ソケット socket (elec)
sokin kawase 送金為替 money order
soko 倉庫 warehouse
sokoni そこに there
sokudo 速度 speed
sokudokei 速度計 speedometer
sokumen 側面 side
someru 染める dye (vb)
sono その the
sonzai suru 存在する be
sora 空 sky
sore それ it (direct object)
soretomo それとも or
sorezore それぞれ each
sori そり sledge
soru 剃る shave
sosa 操作 operation
sosa ソーサー saucer
soseji ソーセージ sausage
soshiki 葬式 funeral
sosogu 注ぐ pour
sosu ソース sauce
soto 外 out
sotogawa 外側 outside
soyokaze そよ風 breeze
su 巣 nest
su 酢 vinegar
subarashii すばらしい excellent, great
suberidai 滑り台 slide (n)
suberiyasui 滑りやすい slippery
suberu 滑る slide (vb), slip
subete 全て everything
suchimu スチーム steam
sudeni すでに already
suedo スエード suede

sugoi すごい amazing, incredible
sugoku ii すごくいい lovely
suguni すぐに immediately, soon, straightaway
suicchi スイッチ switch
suichu yoku 水中翼 hydrofoil
suijyo suki 水上スキー water-skiing
suika スイカ watermelon
suimin 睡眠 sleep
suiminyaku 睡眠薬 sleeping pill
suisen suru 推薦する recommend
suisu スイス Switzerland
suisu jin スイス人 Swiss
suiyobi 水曜日 Wednesday
sukafu スカーフ scarf
sukato スカート skirt
suketo スケート skate (n)
suketo rinku スケートリンク ice rink, skating rink
suketo suru スケートする skate (vb)
suki 好き like (vb)
suki スキー ski (n)
suki butsu スキーブーツ ski boot
suki jampu スキージャンプ ski jump
suki jyo スキー場 ski slope
suki suru スキーする ski (vb)
sukoshi 少し bit, few, a few, little
sukottorando スコットランド Scotland
sukottorando jin スコットランド人 Scot, Scottish
suku u 救う save
sukuname 少なめ less
sukuranburu eggu スクランブルエッグ scrambled eggs
sukurin スクリーン screen
sukyuba daibingu スキューバダイビング scuba diving
sumi 炭 charcoal
sumimasen すみません Excuse me!
sumire スミレ violet
sumoku samon スモークサーモン smoked salmon
sumu 住む live
suna 砂 sand
sunakku スナック snack
sunokeru スノーケル snorkel
supaku puragu スパークプラグ spark plug
supakuringu スパークリング sparkling
supana スパナ spanner
supea patsu スペアパーツ spare part
supea taiya スペアタイヤ spare tyre
supein スペイン Spain
supein jin スペイン人 Spaniard, Spanish
superu スペル spell

supoke スポーク spoke (of wheel)
supongi スポンジ sponge
supongi keki スポンジケーキ sponge cake
suppai 酸っぱい sour
supu スープ soup
supun スプーン spoon
suri すり pickpocket
surippa スリッパ slippers
surobakia jin スロバキア人 Slovak
surobakia kyowakoku スロバキア共和国 Slovak Republic
suru する do
suru tsumori de aru 〜するつもりである intend
surubekidesu 〜するべきです。 should
surudoi 鋭い sharp
surumaeni 〜する前に before
suso すそ hem
sutajiamu スタジアム stadium
sutata スターター starter (car)
sutearingu hoiru ステアリングホイール steering wheel
sutokkingu ストッキング stocking
sutsu スーツ suit
sutsu kesu スーツケース suitcase
suwaru 座る sit
suweden スウェーデン Sweden
suweden jin スウェーデン人 Swedish, Swede
suzumebachi スズメバチ wasp
suzushii 涼しい cool

T

taba 束 bunch
tabako タバコ cigarette
tabemono 食べ物 food
taberu 食べる eat
tabi 旅 journey
tabun たぶん maybe, probably
tabun 多分 perhaps
tachiyoru 立ち寄る stopover
tadashi ただし only, however
tadashii 正しい right
tadashiku 正しく properly
tadasu 正す correct
taeru 耐える tolerate
tafu タフ tough
taiho 逮捕 arrest
taikutsuna 退屈な boring
taipu タイプ type
taira 平ら flat
tairana 平らな even (flat)
taisetsuna 大切な dear
taishikan 大使館 embassy
taitsu タイツ tights
taiya タイヤ tyre
taiya no atsuryoku タイヤの圧力 tyre pressure
taiyo 太陽 sun
taizai 滞在 stay
takai 高い high

takaisu 高椅子 high chair
takasa 高さ height
takkyubin 宅急便 courier service
takujisho 託児所 crèche
takusan たくさん many, much, plenty
takushi タクシー cab, taxi
takushi noriba タクシー乗り場 taxi rank
takushi untenshu タクシー運転手 taxi driver
takuwaeru 蓄える store (vb)
tamago 卵 egg
tamago no kimi 卵の黄身 yolk
tamanegi たまねぎ onion
tamani たまに occasionally
tamesu 試す try
taminaru ターミナル terminal
tampon タンポン tampon
tana 棚 shelf
tani 谷 valley
tanjyobi 誕生日 birthday
tanjyobi kado 誕生日カード birthday card
tanjyobi purezento 誕生日プレゼント birthday present
tanjyunna 単純な simple
tanku タンク cistern, tank
tanoshii 楽しい exciting, fun (adj)
tanoshimi 楽しみ joy
tanoshimu 楽しむ enjoy
tansu たんす chest of drawers
taoru タオル towel
taosu 倒す knock down

tara タラ cod
taru 樽 barrel
tarukamu pauda タルカムパウダー talcum powder
tashika 確か certain, sure
tashikani 確かに certainly
tasukeru 助ける help
tasukete! 助けて！ Help!
tatakai 戦い fight (n)
tatakau 戦う fight (vb)
tatemono 建物 building
tateru 建てる build
tatsu 発つ leave
tawa タワー tower
tawashi たわし scrubbing brush
tazuneru 尋ねる ask
te 手 hand
tebukuro 手袋 gloves
teburu テーブル table
teburu curosu テーブルクロス tablecloth
teburu supun テーブルスプーン tablespoon
teburu wain テーブルワイン table wine
tegami 手紙 letter
tegorona 手ごろな reasonable
teiden 停電 power cut
teido 程度 degree (measurement)
teihaku 停泊 mooring
teiji suru 提示する present (vb)
teikiken 定期券 season ticket

teishi sain 停止サイン stop sign
teishibo 低脂肪 low fat
tekubi 手首 wrist
ten in 店員 shop assistant
teni ireru 手に入れる obtain
tenimotsu 手荷物 baggage, hand luggage
tenimotsu dana 手荷物棚 luggage rack
tenimotsu fuda 手荷物札 luggage tag
tenimotsu uketorijyo 手荷物受取所 baggage reclaim
tenisu テニス tennis
tenisu koto テニスコート tennis court
tenisu raketto テニスラケット tennis racket
tenjikai 展示会 exhibition
tenjyo 天井 ceiling
tenkan てんかん epilepsy
tenkan kanja てんかん患者 epileptic
tenkeitekina 典型的な typical
tenki 天気 weather
tenki no yoi 天気の良い sunny
tenkiyoho 天気予報 weather forecast
tentetsuki 転轍機 points (car)
tento テント tent
tento yo pegu テント用ペグ tent peg

tepu テープ tape
tepu rekoda テープレコーダー tape recorder
tera テーラー tailor
tera 寺 temple
terebi テレビ television
terefon kado テレフォンカード phone card
tetsu 鉄 iron (metal)
tetsudo 鉄道 railway
tezukuri 手作り handmade
ti baggu ティーバッグ tea bag
tipotto ティーポット teapot
tisshu ティッシュ tissue
tisupun ティースプーン teaspoon
to 〜と and
to tomoni 〜と共に with
tobikomidai 飛び込み台 diving board
tobikomu 飛び込む dive
tobu 飛ぶ fly
tochaku 到着 arrival
tochaku suru 到着する arrive
tochi 土地 land
todana 戸棚 cupboard
toge とげ splinter
toge 棘 thorn
toire トイレ toilet
tojikome rareru 閉じ込められる locked in
tojikomeru 閉じ込める lock in
tojyoken 搭乗券 boarding card
tokei 時計 clock
tokeru 溶ける melt

tokeyasui 溶けやすい soluble
toki 陶器 china, pottery
tokidoki 時々 sometimes
toko shorui 渡航書類 travel documents
tokoya 床屋 barber's shop
toku ni 遠くに far (adv)
tokuni 遠くに away
tokuni 特に especially
tomaru 止まる stop
tomato トマト tomato
tomato jusu トマトジュース tomato juice
tomodachi 友達 friend
tonneru トンネル tunnel
tonobyo kanjya 糖尿病患者 diabetic
toppu トップ top
toppuresu トップレス topless
toraberazu chekku トラベラーズチェック traveller's cheque
torakku トラック lorry, truck
toramu トラム tram
toranku トランク trunk (of car)
torei トレイ tray
toreningu uea トレーニングウエア tracksuit
torera トレーラー trailer
tori 鳥 bird
toride 砦 fortress
torihiki 取引 deal
toroku 登録 register (n)
toroku bango 登録番号 registration number
toroku suru 登録する register (vb)
toroku yoshi 登録用紙 registration form
torori トローリー trolley, luggage trolley
toru 取る take
toruko トルコ Turkey
toruko ishi トルコ石 turquoise
toruko jin トルコ人 Turkish, Turk
toshi 年 age, year
toshin 都心 city centre
toshokan 図書館 library
totemo とても very
totsuzen 突然 suddenly
totte 通って through
tottekuru 取ってくる fetch
tozan 登山 mountaineering
tsua opereta ツアーオペレーター tour operator
tsugino 次の next
tsui 対 pair
tsuin beddo ツインベッド twin beds
tsuiyasu 費やす spend (time)
tsuka 通貨 currency
tsukamaeru 捕まえる catch
tsukan 通関 customs
tsukareta 疲れた tired, exhausted
tsukau 使う use
tsukau 使う spend (money)
tsukeru つける switch on
tsuki 月 month, moon
tsukue 机 desk

tsukurareta 作られた made
tsukuru 作る make
tsuma 妻 wife
tsumasaki 爪先 toe
tsumatta 詰まった stuffed
tsume 爪 nail
tsume burashi 爪ブラシ nail brush
tsume yasuri 爪やすり nail file
tsumekiri 爪きり nail scissors
tsumemono 詰め物 filling (tooth)
tsumetai 冷たい cold
tsuno 角 horn (animal)
tsurino kyoka 釣りの許可 fishing permit
tsurizao 釣り竿 fishing rod
tsuro 通路 aisle
tsurogawa no seki 通路側の席 aisle seat
tsutsumu 包む pack, wrap up
tsuyakusha 通訳者 interpreter
tsuyoi 強い strong
tuskaisute omutsu 使い捨てオムツ disposable diapers/nappies

U
ubaguruma 乳母車 pushchair
uchigawa 内側 inside
udedokei 腕時計 watch (n)
udedokei no beruto 腕時計のベルト watch strap
ue 上 above
ue e 上へ up
uekiya 植木屋 nursery (plants)
uesuto ウエスト waist
uettosutsu ウェットスーツ wetsuit
ugai うがい mouthwash
ugoku 動く move
ujimushi 蛆虫 maggot
uketorinin 受取人 receiver (tax)
uketoru 受け取る accept
uketsuke 受付 reception
uketsuke gakari 受付係り receptionist
uketsukejyo 受付所 enquiry desk
uma 馬 horse
umaretsukino 生まれつきの born
umi 海 ocean, sea
un 運 luck
unagi うなぎ eel
unchin 運賃 fare
unga 運河 canal
unten menkyo 運転免許 driving licence
unten suru 運転する drive
untenshu 運転手 driver
ureshi うれしい glad
uru 売る sell
uru ウール wool
urusai うるさい loud, noisy
usagi ウサギ rabbit
ushi 牛 cow

uso 嘘 lie (n)
uso wo tsuku 嘘をつく lie (vb)
usu yogorete 薄汚れて dinghy
uta 歌 song
utau 歌う sing
utsu 打つ hit, strike
utsukushii 美しい beautiful
uwanuri 上塗り overcoat
uweb ウェブ web
uweita / uweitoresu ウェイター / ウェイトレス waiter/waitress
uweruzu ウェールズ Wales
uweruzu, uweruzujin dansei, uweru zujin jyosei ウェールズ、ウェールズ人男性、ウェールズ人女性 Welsh, Welshman, Welshwoman
uwin ウィーン Vienna
uwirusu ウィルス virus

W
wa 輪 ring, circle
wain ワイン wine
wain batake ワイン畑 vineyard
wain gurasu ワイングラス wine glass
waiya ワイヤー wire
wakai 若い young
wakareru 別れる separate
wakuchin ワクチン vaccine
wan 湾 bay
wara わら straw
waraigoe 笑い声 laugh (n)

warau 笑う laugh (vb)
waribiki 割引 discount
warui 悪い bad
washi 鷲 eagle
wasuremono 忘れ物 lost property
wasureru 忘れる forget
watashi 私 me, myself
watashi no 私の my
Watashi wa ...desu 私は〜です。 I am
watashitachi 私たち us, we
watashitachi no 私たちの our
wo imi suru 〜を意味する mean (intend)
wo konomu 〜を好む prefer
wo mochiageru 〜を持ち上げる lift

Y
yabu 藪 bush
yabureteiru 破れている torn
yaburu 破る tear (vb)
yagate やがて eventually
yagi ヤギ goat
yakan やかん kettle
yakkyoku 薬局 chemist, pharmacy
yaku 約 about (approximately)
yaku 焼く burn
yakugaku 薬学 medicine (science)
yakusoku 約束 date, appointment, promise (n)
yakusoku suru 約束する promise (vb)

yakuzaishi 薬剤師 pharmacist
yama 山 mountain
yane 屋根 roof
yaneura 屋根裏 attic
yaoya 八百屋 greengrocer's
yarisugi やり過ぎ overdone
yasai 野菜 vegetables
yaseta 痩せた thin
yasui 安い cheap
yasui nedan 安い値段 cheap rate
yasumi 休み holidays
yasuri やすり file (tool)
yawarakai やわらかい soft
yoake 夜明け dawn
yobidashi 呼び出し call (vb)
yobun no 余分の extra
yodoshi no 夜通しの overnight
yofukudansu 洋服ダンス wardrobe
yogoreta 汚れた dirty
yoi 良い fine, good, well
yoi ga dekite 用意ができて ready
yoi suru 用意をする arrange
yoji 楊枝 toothpick
yoko ni naru 横になる lie down
yokushitsu 浴室 bathroom
yomu 読む read
yon bun no ichi 4分の1 quarter
yonku 四駆 four-wheel drive
yori shitani 〜より下に below

yori toku e より遠くへ further
yoriito より糸 thread
yorimichi 寄り道 detour
yoriyoi より良い better
yorokobaseru 喜ばせる please
yorokobu 喜ぶ pleased
yoroppa ヨーロッパ Europe
yoroppa jin ヨーロッパ人 European
yoru 夜 night
yosei 要請 request (n)
yosei suru 要請する request (vb)
yoshi 用紙 form (document), sheet
yotsu 腰痛 backache
yotta 酔った drunk
yotto ヨット yacht
yowai 弱い weak
yoyaku 予約 reservation
yoyaku suru 予約する reserve
yube 夕べ last night
yubi 指 finger
yubin 郵便 mail (n)
yubin bako 郵便箱 postbox
yubin bango 郵便番号 postal code
yubin de okuru 郵便で送る post (vb)
yubin ryokin 郵便料金 postage
yubin uke 郵便受け letterbox
yubinkyoku 郵便局 post office
yubinkyokuin 郵便局員 postman/postwoman
yubiwa 指輪 ring

yudayakyoto, yudayajin ユダヤ教徒、ユダヤ人 Jew, Jewish
yude ゆで boil (n)
yuderu ゆでる boil (vb)
yufukuna 裕福な rich
yugata 夕方 evening
yuiitsu no 唯一の only
yuka 床 floor (of room)
yukai 愉快 fun (n)
yukazokin 床雑巾 floorcloth
yuki 雪 snow
yuki ga futteiru 雪が降っている it is snowing
yukisaibai yasai 有機栽培野菜 organic vegetables
yukkuri ゆっくり slowly
yuko 有効 valid
yumei 有名 famous
yumoa ユーモア humour
yureru 揺れる swing
yurui ゆるい loose
yurusu 許す allow
yuryodoro 有料道路 toll, toll road
yushoku 夕食 dinner, supper
yushutsu suru 輸出する export
yuso suru 郵送する mail (vb)
yusu hosuteru ユースホステル youth hostel
yutampo 湯たんぽ hot-water bottle

Z
zairyo 材料 ingredients
zannen 残念 pity, It's a pity!
zasshi 雑誌 magazine
zei 税 tax
zeitakuhin 贅沢品 luxury
zenbu 全部 whole (n)
zenmugi pan 全麦パン wholemeal bread
zentai de 全体で altogether
zeri ゼリー jelly
zero ゼロ zero
zettai shinai 絶対しない never
zettaini 絶対に definitely, absolutely
zo 像 statue
zokin 雑巾 rag
zon ゾーン zone
zubon ズボン trousers
zubon shita ズボン下 underpants
zuimakuen 髄膜炎 meningitis
zukin 頭巾 hood (garment)
zutsu 頭痛 headache